Broussard's

RESTAURANT & COURTYARD COOKBOOK

Broussard's

RESTAURANT & COURTYARD COOKBOOK

Ann Benoit

and

The Preuss Family

PELICAN PUBLISHING COMPANY

GRETNA 2012

ISBN 9781455614899

Copy Edited by Shawn Ringen

Printed in China
Published by Pelican Publishing Company, Inc.
1000 Burmaster Street, Gretna, La. 70053

by Evelyn & Gunter Preuss

With love for our sons, Marc and Andreas
and Evelyn's sister, Ingrid.

by Marc Preuss

With love for my family.

by Ann Benoit

To two extraordinary women.
Each had the vision to see a new life and the courage to make it a real.
Evelyn Preuss and Kit Wohl

And

To two extraordinary men of vision and courage,
Tom Dalferes and Bob Rintz
each gives freely in time, kindness, belief and support
and each, as always, knows who he is.

A WALK THROUGH BROUSSARD'S

The first time I walked through the unique tiled foyer of Broussard's into the dining room on its courtyard, one word came to my mind: romance.

The year was 1975, and famed local restaurant architect Charles Gresham's new design had just been revealed to the public. After fifty years of dining at the old Broussard's, New Orleans had a dazzling new Broussard's.

The transformation disproved a widely-held myth. It was believed that the French Quarter's grande dame restaurants—of which Broussard's is unambiguously one—could not be changed in looks, menu, or service style without upsetting all the customers. The crowds that filled the reincarnated Broussard's showed otherwise. The success of Broussard's encouraged Arnaud's, Galatoire's, and Antoine's to follow suit sooner or later.

Broussard's was an able accomplice in my young dating years. The ladies I dined with there took on a glow I didn't often see elsewhere. Maybe it was the flattering lighting. Or the courtyard—the most expansive of any French Quarter restaurant. The elegant and wonderful food and service surely helped.

All that was enhanced when Chef Gunter and Evelyn Preuss took over Broussard's in the 1980s. Evelyn, acting as tastemaker, never thought it enough to be merely beautiful. Glamorous was a more interesting goal, as she proved every day by just showing up at Broussard's.

Meanwhile, her chef husband continued to pursue the polish that has attended his food throughout his nearly fifty years of cooking in New Orleans. A chef like Gunter knows that tastes change, and he has encouraged his chefs de cuisine to break out of the traditions where the results would be gratifying. Over the years they've created a new cuisine for Broussard's that refers to the glorious past without being stuck in it.

Broussard's has entered yet another new era as the Preusses' son Marc—part of the restaurant for over twenty years—takes over management. No doubt it will be yet another new Broussard's when the grand restaurant celebrates its first century in 2020.

Tastefully yours,
Tom Fitzmorris
New Orleans, Louisiana

Broussard's RESTAURANT & COURTYARD COOKBOOK
CREOLE CREATIVITY IN THE FRENCH QUARTER

TABLE OF CONTENTS

INTRODUCTION

A *capriccio* is an architectural fantasy, placing together buildings and other architectural elements to create a fictional fantasy. Broussard's is both a *capriccio*, and a *bella maniera*, art mimicking art, where presentation of the object is as important as the object itself. Every element of Broussard's is an allegorical or historical reference. Everything has a meaning. Nothing is left to chance and items may be more than they appear.

"It was all done intentionally," says Mr. Joe Segreto, the leader of the renovation that gave us Broussard's.

The ceramic tiles, the Venetian masks, the design of the chandeliers, the painting on the cabinetry, all have their own elusive meaning, their own historical message reaching back into time. Indeed, the predominate colors of the three dining rooms - white in the Napoleon Room, green in the Josephine Room and red in the Magnolia Room are the colors of the Italian flag.

Bella maniera art imitating art.

Broussard's is itself a work of art.

THE PREUSS FAMILY

With the Preuss family it is hard to know where one ends and the other begins, so seamless are their interactions. Evelyn and Gunter team up for the morning shift, readying the stage for the night, leaving when Marc bursts onto the scene to run the evenings -- a division of time and labor that defines the style of this trio. With Chef Preuss as substance, Mrs. Preuss as style and Mr. Preuss as the future, all complimenting each other beautifully, this trio of restaurateurs is sure to continue as they are for years to come.

GUNTER PREUSS

Chef Gunter Preuss is a second-generation restaurateur, trained in the European system. Chef Preuss' apprenticeship began at a health spa in West Germany. From there he progressed to the famous Palace Hotel in St. Moritz, also working in Sweden, to round out his education, before arriving at the Mission Hills Country Club in Kansas City. The New York Statler Hilton soon offered Chef Preuss a position. He was then promoted to Executive Chef of the Statler Hilton in Washington D.C. Further promotion and success followed when Chef Preuss was offered a position as Executive Chef and Food & Beverage Director at the Fairmont in New Orleans. In 1972 the Preusses opened the Versailles, bringing Continental Cuisine to the city.

When the historically significant Broussard's became available, Chef and Mrs. Preuss brought their expertise and experience to the historic Creole establishment. "We have built our lives around the restaurant," say both Chef and Mrs. Preuss.

Although Pope John Paul II visited many New Orleans restaurants in his September 10-21, 1987 official Papal visit to the United States, few New Orleanians realize that only Chef Gunter Preuss of Broussard's was trusted with the daily preparation of all of His Holinesses in-residence meals.

Chef Preuss was the team leader for "the United States Culinary Olympics" team which won a Gold medal in the Pan American Culinary competition.

Profiled on the original "Great Chefs of New Orleans" series for PBS, Chef Preuss is the recipient of both the Mobile Guide and the Holiday Travel Awards.

Cornell University's School of Hotel Administration, acknowledged as one of the best in the country, awarded Chef Preuss and Broussard's the Cornell University Fine Dining Award.

The Ivy Award by Restaurants & Institutions Magazine is one of the most coveted awards in the industry with only 6 Ivy Awards are given per year. Broussard's is an Ivy Award recipient.

Only 800 restaurants in the United States are recipients of the DiRoNa award. Broussard's has been a DiRoNa, Distinguished Restaurants of North America Achievement of Distinction in Dining Award, winner every single year.

Broussard's is named to the prestigious Fine Dining Hall of Fame by Nation's Restaurant News.

Chef Preuss is instrumental in establishing national standards for local cuisine through the introduction of national organizations. Chef Preuss is the first President and founder of the local chapter of the American Culinary Federation and a member of the American Academy of Chefs. He was instrumental in bringing Les Chaines de Rotisseurs to New Orleans and served as Vice Conseiller de Culinaire.

Consistently serving the community and mentoring the next generation of chefs, Chef Preuss is a founding member of the Chefs Charity for Children. A sell-out every year, this tremendously successful fundraiser supports St. Michael's Special School for children and young adults with developmental disabilities. In recent years, stars from the Food Network have come to New Orleans to participate in this worthy event.

Chef Preuss served as an Executive Board Member of both the Greater New Orleans Tourist & Convention Commission and the Louisiana Restaurant Association. He has served as Director of the New Orleans Food Festival and a Chef Instructor at both the Delgado Community College Culinary Program and the John Folse Culinary Institute at Nicholls State University.

EVELYN PREUSS

As Gunter Preuss is substance, so Evelyn Preuss is force plus style.

Vision, determination, and intelligence define Mrs. Preuss. Born, raised and educated in Berlin, Evelyn wanted to live in America and made it happen. In 1960 Chef and Mrs. Preuss arrived in Kansas City, moving through increasingly finer hotels and restaurants. Evelyn located the property for the Versailles and supported Gunter in the risky jump of opening his own business. With an iron will, nerves of steel and an unshakable belief in her husband, Mrs. Preuss became the "front of the house." Evelyn and Gunter opened the Versailles, bringing the Preusses to the forefront of the New Orleans restaurant world. When Broussard's became available they had already established themselves as one of New Orleans premier restaurant teams. Everyone knew the Preusses would succeed --- and they have.

MARC PREUSS

Marc Preuss is co-owner and General Manager. A restaurateur and hospitality professional by experience and education, he was awarded a Bachelor's Degree in Hotel/Restaurant Administration from the Salzburger Hotel School in Bad Hofgastein, Austria. Mr. Preuss completed externships at both the Fairmont Hotel and the famed Hotel Rhodaniain in Verbier Switzerland, an all French-speaking establishment.

Marc Preuss embarked on his career, taking major leadership roles in some of the world's finest establishments including The Ritz Carlton Hotel and The Sun International Resorts Palace Hotel in South Africa.

As would be expected of a son of Gunter and Evelyn, Marc began learning the restaurant and hospitality industry at a young age. His experience, energy and stamina earn him respect among his peers and colleagues. Today, Mr. Preuss continues to focus on delivering the highest service standards to complement Broussard's tradition and his family legacy, combining his Father's substance with his Mother's tour de force and making it all uniquely his own.

A PAPAL VISIT: CRAWFISH BROUSSARD

SERVES 6

2   Tablespoons Fresh butter

2   Tablespoons sliced Green onions

1   Tablespoon minced French
    shallots

2   teaspoons minced Garlic

1/2 cup White wine

1/4 Lemon, juiced

1 3/4 cups Béchamel sauce *[recipe
    p.194]*

1 1/2 Tablespoons fresh Dill

1 1/2 pounds boiled Crawfish tails

Salt

Cayenne

1/2 cup freshly grated Parmigiano-
    Reggiano

6   boiled Crawfish tails

Although Pope John Paul II visited many New Orleans restaurants in September of 1987, few New Orleanians realize that only Gunter Preuss of Broussard's was trusted with the daily preparation of all of His Holinesses in-residence meals.

Enjoy with a Pinot Blanc and the heavenly sounds of the St. Louis Cathedral Young Artist in Residence, a program jointly established in 2009 by the Paris Conservatory and the St. Louis Cathedral music program. Dating from 1720, the St. Louis Cathedral Music Program is one of the oldest continually operating music programs in the United States.

Preheat oven to 350 degrees F.

In a medium saucepan over medium heat, melt butter. Add onions, shallots, and garlic and sauté until transparent, but not brown, about 2 minutes. Add wine and lemon juice and reduce by half. Add Béchamel Sauce and reduce by one-third. Add crawfish and simmer for 10 minutes. Season to taste with salt and cayenne. Put in ramekins, top with Parmigiano-Reggiano and bake in oven until cheese is golden brown and bubbly. Garnish with crawfish and serve immediately.

THE HISTORY OF BROUSSARD'S

Broussard's location at 819 Conti Street has a long and distinguished place in the history of the City of New Orleans.

What is now Broussard's was on Bienville's first plan for the City of New Orleans. Conti Street is one of the streets on the 11 block by 7 block original rectangular plan for the Vieux Carré. The original map, located in the Library of Congress, indicates that in 1722 the property was assigned to Dr. P. Delatour, Surgeon for the French Crown assigned to the colony.

The December 1731 Gonichon map in the "Archives Nationales Colonies" in Paris indicates the Cognon property was by then fenced and owned by Louis Francois LaRoche Castel.

Meanwhile, Joseph Broussard dit Beausoleil, anti-British fighter and the General of the Acadian resistance in Nova Scotia arrived in Louisiana with a large group of over 200 family and affiliated members in February of 1765. In April of that same year, the Broussard's entered into the Dauterive Compact with Atakapas cattleman Jean Antoine Bernard Dauterive to settle his land grant and to tend his livestock for a part of the profit. French army engineer Louis Antoine Andry led the Broussards across the Atchafalaya Basin. The Broussard's established the area that eventually came to be known as the town of Loreauville. Joseph Broussard dit Beausoleil was named Capitaine Commandant des Acadiens aux Atakapas by French Interim Governor Charles-Philippe Aubry. The Broussard's were gifted cattlemen, soon growing to be a power in the Louisiana livestock industry, and in later years often supplied beef to restaurants.

In 1827 Samuel Hermann purchased the Conti St. property, which he owned until 1842. The Conti Street property joined his St. Louis Street property at the rear line.

Sometime during this period, possibly 1834, Hermann built what is today the Josephine Room and the Magnolia Room with its second floor and balcony. Judge Felix Grima next acquired the property. The Hermann-Grima House at 820 St. Louis St., like Broussard's, is today on the National Historic Register. The Hermann-Grima House offers historically accurate cooking demonstrations in its 1830's outdoor Creole kitchen.

Destiny continued to twine the strands of city and country. In 1891 Joseph Cesar Broussard was born in Loreauville. His brother Robert was born in Loreauville in 1901. The next year, Joseph Broussard went to New Orleans to earn his fame and fortune in the restaurant business. He prospered and was promoted often by his employers, but wishing to learn more, he entered the French apprentice system and paid to be trained under Chef Mornay Voiron at the Restaurant Durand in Paris. He returned to New Orleans, created many new recipes, and met the beautiful Rosalie Borello. Joseph and Rosalie were married at St. Louis Cathedral and had their reception at the Borello home, the first of many held at 819 Conti. Rosalie's parents, Anthony Borello and Mary Ann Guarino Borello gave the Conti property's use to the young couple as a wedding present. With his beautiful young bride by his side, Joseph and Rosalie opened Broussard's in 1920, residing in the upstairs apartments. The style of Rosalie and Joseph Broussard's restaurant, like their marriage, successfully blended and celebrated two cultures: the Sicilian and the French. Immediately successful, Joseph sent for his younger brother Robert to help in the business. Robert moved into the vacant apartments over the Magnolia Room and promptly fell in love with and married Rosalie's beautiful younger sister, Philomena. The 1930 Census shows that Joseph,

Rosalie, Robert, Philomena and their six year old daughter Phyllis all lived at 819 Conti St. Joseph died in 1966 at the age of 76. Like all true lovers, he and Rosalie died within a year of each other. Rosalie and Joseph left an enduring stamp on New Orleans culinary history.

In 1974 the dynamic team of Owner and General Partner Joseph Segreto and Partners Joseph Marcello, Jr. and Joseph C. Marcello, purchased the property and began a massive restoration. Mr. Segreto, an experienced restaurateur with a series of successes to his credit, including the Elmwood Plantation, the Red Onion, Shadows Plantation on the Northshore and the discerning Eleven 79, directed the restoration. He created something both wholly original and classically beautiful, "The Restaurant as Art."

The Preuss family continues and expands the tradition of Broussard's into and beyond its 100th year.

THE FOYER

Entering the Central Foyer of Broussard's one is immediately taken by its beauty. Though a pedestrian hallway, it is a grand entrance to the dining experience before one. The high ceiling is beamed with antique sinker cypress. The custom designed sconces and chandelier of iron and porcelain tulips echo a history of their own and the extensive tile work all speak... this is no ordinary place.

About the four walls are custom designed hand painted tiles by New Orleans artist Charles Reinike. The tiles feature "putti" or cherubs, a popular motif during the Renaissance. The putti on Broussard's walls are an intentional reference to the putti on the Fontaine des Innocents in Place Joachim-du-Bellay in the Les Halles district of the 1st arrondissement of Paris. It is the oldest monumental fountain in Paris and the last Renaissance fountain in Paris. Pierre Lescot, the architect of the fountain, also worked on the Louvre, bringing Italian Renaissance style to Paris. Built to commemorate Henry II's royal entrance into Paris, the fountain did not have sufficient water until Napoleon built an aqueduct from the River Ourcq. The Fontaine des

Innocents is adorned with both Renaissance putti and Mannerist bas relief. Just as the Fontaine des Innocents welcomed Henry II to Paris, so the putti, who are all in the process of preparing a meal, welcome our guests to

Broussard's. Above the doorway is the legend "Soyez bienvenus chez Broussard." Welcome to the house of Broussard.

The sconces and chandeliers in the Foyer and in the Magnolia Room were done in the fashion of the iron tulips of Marie Antoinette. Marie Antoinette's sister Maria Carolina of Austria was the Queen of Naples and Sicily as the wife of King Ferdinand. Maria Carolina and Marie Antoinette were very close. While reigning as Queen of France, Marie Antoinette missed the tulip of her native land and sought to have them grown at Versailles. They did not do well, so Marie commisioned tulips made of gold. Le Petit Trianon was ransacked during the French Revolution, but replicas of the gold tulips can be seen today in her restored bedroom in Le Petit Trianon. As a ruler, Maria Carolina had practiced enlightened absolutism or benevolent dictatorship over her domains of Naples and Sicily, which allowed for religious tolerance, freedom of speech, freedom of the press, and private property ownership all before the French Revolution. When Napoleon won Naples, Maria Carolina and her family escaped to Sicily. Iron and porcelain tulips made into sconces and chandeliers are a reminder Marie Antoinette and Maria Carolina, France and Sicily, like te family of Joseph Broussard.

Presiding over all is the legend: *"Soyez bienvenu chez Broussard."* "You are welcomed to the house of Broussard."

THE HISTORIC RENOVATION OF BROUSSARD'S

The demolition took 3 months, the renovation - 23, all the while continuing and expanding the two cultural traditions established by Rosalie and Joseph Broussard.

Assembled was the team of Samuel Wilson, Jr., Architect, Charles Gresham, Designer and Charles Reinike, Artist all under the aegis of Mr. Joe Segreto, General Partner and Co-Owner of Broussard's.

SAMUEL WILSON, JR., ARCHITECT

Samuel Wilson, Jr. is often referred to as "The Dean of Historic Preservation." A graduate of Warren Easton High School and Tulane University's School of Architecture, his career included rehabilitation or restoration of many projects, including the Cabildo, Shadows-On-The-Teche plantation, the Pontalba Buildings, the Ursuline Convent, San Francisco plantation, St. Patrick's Church, Gallier House, the Hermann-Grima House, the Rene Beauregard House, Trinity Church, St. Mary's Assumption Church, the French Market, Pitot House, Dillard University, Works Progress Administration projects in City Park including the golf house, the pigeonnieres, shelters, bridges, gardens and the stadium, Feibleman Department Store which became Sears, the American Bank Building, the many properties of General Lewis Kemper Williams and Mrs. Leila Hardie Moore Williams now known as the Historic New Orleans Collection, the House on Ellicott Hill, King's Tavern, Magnolia Hall, and, of course, Broussard's. Married to the great-great-grand-daughter of Benjamin Henry Latrobe, the Father of American Architecture, who designed the U.S. Capitol in Washington DC and the US Customs House in New Orleans, among others. Wilson edited *Impressions Respecting New Orleans* by Benjamin Henry Bonval Latrobe in 1951. Samuel Wilson published hundreds of papers during his career and taught the course "Historic Louisiana Architecture" for 38 years at Tulane University. He helped to found many organizations including Friends of the Cabildo, the Louisiana Landmarks Society, the Preservation Resource Center, the Orleans Parish Landmarks Commission, and Save Our Cemeteries.

CHARLES GRESHAM, DESIGNER

Renowned New Orleans Designer Charles Gresham was regularly an essential part of a Wilson team. With a breathtakingly expansive knowledge of period design, Charles Gresham's work included, not only Broussard's, but also the New Orleans Country Club, Brennan's on Royal Street, The Zemurray House at Number 2 Audubon Place, Commander's Palace and the 13th century Castle of the Knights of Malta in Italy, as well as many of the Sam Wilson projects.

CHARLES REINIKE, ARTIST

Charles Reinike and his team consisting of his son Charles Reinike III and his wife Vera were often involved in Wilson projects. Mr. Reinike's works have been exhibited at the Smithsonian, the New Orleans Museum of Art, Columbia University and the Ogden Museum of Southern Art among others and today are highly sought by collectors.

Born in New Orleans in 1906, Mr. Reinike was educated at the Gradham School of Art in New Orleans and the Chicago Academy of Fine Arts where he met fellow artist and his future wife, Vera Hefter of Hamburg, West Germany. They married and returned to New Orleans, starting the Reinike Academy of Art at 630 Toulouse St. at the Governor William Charles Cole Claiborne House. In the 1930s they opened Reinike Gallery. During World War II, Charles Reinike worked at Higgins Industries in New Orleans, famous for the design and construction of the Higgins boat. A Higgins Boat and the story of Higgins Industries is on permanent exhibit in The National World War II Museum in New Orleans. After the War, Charles and Vera raised their three children, Audrey, Gretchen and Charles III and pursued active careers in commissioned art, as well as operating Reinike Gallery. The Reinike's offered an Art Retreat in

legendary murals in the Caribbean Room Restaurant and The Bayou Bar of the Pontchartrain Hotel, the murals at both New Orleans Country Club and Metairie Country Club, and the murals at Vista Shore Country Club, to name but a few.

Many historic homes at New Orleans' best addresses, St. Charles Avenue, Audubon Place, Exposition Boulevard, Nashville, Vincent Avenue and Prytania, house commissioned murals by the Reinikes. The Center Hall of the exquisite Maddox-McClendon House at 2507 Prytania Street, already endowed with its own private ballroom, is graced with a mural of trailing vines and butterflies by Vera Reinike as well as a hidden garden where putti enjoy a fountain.

Reinike Gallery, now located in Atlanta, continues a close association with New Orleans' best. The New Orleans Opera Association chose Charles Reinike III to create the painting for the 2010 Opera Ball. One can enjoy the Reinike "putti" or cherubs, a national treasure adorning The Central Foyer at Broussard's.

St. Francisville, Louisiana at their camp Audubon Woods. An oil by Vera is located in Greenwood Plantation in St. Francisville in West Feliciana Parish and Reinike art is to be found in many plantation homes in the area.

Much of New Orleans that is notable is adorned by the Reinikes. The Pickwick Club, founded in 1857 is one of the oldest private clubs in continuous existence in the United States. Charles Reinike executed the Pickwick Club murals during its 1950 renovation. Other Vera or Charles or Charles III Reinike commissions include the mosaics and murals in Our Lady of Guadeloupe Chapel, the murals, windows, and stations of the cross at the Mercy Hospital Chapel, a bas-relief at Lake Lawn Mausoleum, for which Charles III's wife Edna modeled, the pewter bas relief inlay in pecan of The Tree of Life at Temple Sinai which was Charles III's design, the pewter bas relief of New Orleans and Louisiana Fish and Fowl at the Bon Ton Café, the enamel on copper Tree of Life designed by Charles III as lead artist at Congregation Gates of Prayer in Metairie, the mural at Our Lady of Prompt Succor Church, the

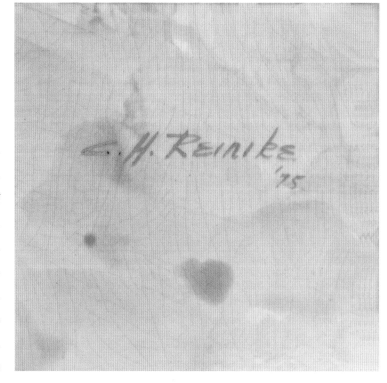

THE NAPOLEON ROOM

The French Empire style takes its name from Napoleon's Empire and is the second phase of the Neoclassical design movement. Napoleon sought to characterize his reign as a return to the glory of the classical Roman periods. With its more masculine and simplified lines, Empire is an elegant response to the excesses of the French Rococo style, the style of the Monarchs. More importantly, the Empire style served to remind the French people of Napoleon's successes by inclusion of arrows and other implements of war as motifs. Egyptian figures as ormolu served as a reminder of his Egyptian campaign. Napoleon's personal symbol, the bee surrounded by a laurel wreath was used liberally. The Empire style is propaganda in furniture. Through the French Empire style, which in fashion included lightweight simple dresses without corsets, Napoleon sought to remind the people that he had liberated them and brought them an Empire as grand as the Roman empire.

The Napoleon Dining room is decorated in the Empire Style. The molding on the intersecting rafters is egg and dart molding with an arrow motif for the dart. Crystal chandeliers were popularized in the Empire style and the Napoleon Room sconces are classic Empire-style with ormolu, shaped like a plummeting hot air balloon. Napoleon commissioned a hot air balloon from Andre Garnerin as part of the event at which Napoleon crowned himself Emperor in 1804. The balloon had a huge golden crown on top. Two days after the event, the balloon, having made its way to Rome, snagged the crown on Nero's tomb, Rome's worst Emperor, and crashed into Lake Bracciano. Hot air balloons were used in the Napoleonic Wars and by the French in the siege of Paris in 1870. The chandeliers in the Napoleon Room were custom designed by Charles Gresham and fabricated by a well-known Royal Street antique shop specializing in chandeliers, using the black and gold crown design associated with the period. A similar entirely gold Second Empire chandelier is located in the Red Room at the White House. The ornate gold mirrors in the Napoleon Room are also Empire.

Ornamenting the walls of the Napoleon Room are antique Venetian masks of the *commedia dell'arte*, the professional improvisational theater that flourished during the Mannerist period and gave rise to Punch and Judy, Shakespeare, Moliere, vaudeville, slapstick, the soap opera, burlesque and opera. Pulcinella is a prominent Neapolitan commedia dell'arte character. The famous Gelosi *commedia del Arte* troop used the symbol of Janus, the god of comings and goings to signify its travels to and from Venice during the carnival season and was composed of 10 stock characters. The walls of Broussard's are adorned with the traditional 10 classic masks of *commedia dell'arte*.

The circular reliefs in the doorway of the Napoleon Room are in the style of the famous Capodimonte porcelain factory established in Naples in 1743 by the Bourbon King Charles. The Palace of Capodimonte Reggia di Capodimonte in Naples was the summer residence of the king of the Two Sicilies, Ferdinand I, the husband of Maria Carolina, Marie Antoinette's sister. Napoleon's brother Joseph and later his brother-in-law Joachim Murat occupied the Palace of Capodimonte for 10 year until Ferdinand returned from Sicily in 1815.

The Empire-style dining chairs in the Napoleon Room were custom designed for the room and manufactured by fine furniture manufacturer Shelby-Williams. The chair proved so popular with Broussard's customers, who often inquired where they could obtain one, that soon the manufacturer offered the custom design for retail sale. Covered in luxurious

In the Napoleon Room...

...a Wedding

white leather on the front and a neoclassical stripe on the back, the chairs are on casters so perfectly balanced that a waiter may slide a lady's chair in and out using only one finger. Both gentlemen's' chairs with arms and ladies' chairs without arms are tableside.

Moving from European history to New Orleans history, centered in the Napoleon Room is a massive white illuminated wine cabinet which was originally located in New Orleans famous St. Charles Hotel at 201 St. Charles Avenue. Canova's sculpture of George Washington was located in the lobby of the St. Charles Hotel, which served as a meeting place for Presidents and Kings. Purchased at auction, the cabinet was raised and custom fitted to the Napoleon room.

New Orleans heat created a New Orleans dining tradition. Until the advent of universal air conditioning, a glass of ice water was always wordlessly served at a diner's place immediately upon seating. To prevent excess waiter traffic into the kitchen and to keep waiters close and attentive to their patrons, an ice and water station was built in Broussard's main dining room.

Many modern restaurants have dispensed with service plates to their detriment. Service plates serve both an ornamental and a practical purpose. As the service plate stays on the table, the waiter immediately knows where a chair should go and where to put a dinner plate. At Broussard's each dining room has its own style of service plate used only in that room, a glamorous touch.

At the far end of the Napoleon Room, antique French doors were added for a view of the beautiful courtyard. Creole patio doors were narrower than those fabricated today. A bank of three pairs of doors open to the courtyard. Slightly further on the same wall, a pair of antique wood paneled doors serve as the entry to the historic Josephine room.

BOURBON-MARINATED CELERIC SALAD

SERVES 6

2 to 3 Whole celeriac [celery root], scrubbed

MARINADE

3/4 cup Olive oil

1/4 cup Bourbon

1/2 cup Sliced green onions

1/2 Medium white onion, sliced

Salt

White Pepper

DRESSING

1/4 cup Chopped green onions

1/4 cup Pickles

1/4 cup Chopped pimento

1 Tablespoon Chopped shallots

1 Tablespoon Chopped parsley

1 Tablespoon Capers

2 Tablespoons Bourbon

1 teaspoon Chopped garlic

1/2 cup Salad oil

3 cups Arugula

1 cup Buttered Cayenne Pecans
   [recipe p.197]

Blue Cheese

WITH SPICED PECANS AND BOURBON-SHALLOT VINAIGRETTE
- A BROUSSARD'S CUSTOM RECIPE

While any restaurant can present a pre-planned catering menu, Broussard's is one of the very few capable of Custom Designed Recipes, such as this recipe originally created for a wedding held at Broussard's. The bride wished to honor her grandparents with a special dish—her Cajun grandmother with spicy pecans and her Kentucky grandfather, a Bourbon man. So successful was the recipe that the following year, Broussard's reintroduced it with Broussard's Bourbon, Blue Jeans & Blues Dinner, combining the music of New Orleans own bluesmaster Walter "Wolfman" Washington, an Historical Whiskey Narrative and a five course custom designed recipe menu featuring bourbon in every course. Don't miss it next year!

At the Blues dinner, this dish was paired with a California Chardonnay and, of course, the blues of Walter "Wolfman" Washington.

In a large stockpot, boil whole scrubbed celery root in lightly salted water until fork tender, about 20 minutes. Remove from water and cool completely. Peel celeriac, removing all eyes and traces of brown skin. Cut crosswise in half and then lengthwise into 1/4 inch slices. In a 2 quart glass baking dish, layer celeriac slices.

To make marinade, combine olive oil, bourbon, green onions, white onions and salt and pepper to taste. Pour marinade over celeric, moving slices to allow some marinade underneath. Marinate overnight, 8-12 hours.

To make dressing, combine all ingredients in a two cup glass jar and shake. Refrigerate. Shake before using.

To plate, toss arugula in dressing. Center arugula on plate. Place two slices of celeriac atop arugula. Drizzle dressing in a line across center of arugula. Garnish with blue cheese and pecans.

Note: Cauliflower may be substituted for celeriac but do not substitute olive oil for salad oil as olive oil is heavier and "weighs down" the delicacy of the vinaigrette.

...*Mardi Gras*

Nicola, Brandon, Charlotte and Lele.

LE BOEUF GRAS

SERVES 6

2   6-ounce Veal filets, flattened

1/4 cup New Orleans style brown
      mustard

1 1/2 pound Beef tenderloin,
      flattened

1/2 teaspoon Chopped garlic

1/2 teaspoon Dried thyme

3   Tablespoons Cooking oil

1   cup White wine

2   Tablespoons Chopped shallots

1/4 teaspoon Thyme

1/2 Bay leaf

2   cups Brown Sauce Number 2
      [recipe p.196]

1   Tablespoon Fresh tarragon

1   Tablespoon Fresh butter

Salt

Freshly ground black pepper

Broussard's extravagant dish of beef literally "fattened" or "stuffed" with veal honors Le Boeuf Gras. Le Boeuf Gras, the Fatted Oxen, is always an early float in the Rex parade on Mardi Gras morning, but has a much older history. Druids during the Fête de Soleil walked a fatted oxen strewn with flower garlands to its sacrifice and the celebratory feasting of the clan. The Romans adopted the custom as did Catholicism in 1512, incorporating the custom into the last extravagant meat meal before Lent. Today the French medieval town of Bazas, 45 minutes southeast of Bordeaux, is famous for its Fête du Boeuf Gras on Mardi Gras day.

Savor this dish with a Pinot Noir while listening to Bobby Lounge's version of I See the Parade.

Season veal with salt, pepper and one-fourth of the mustard. In a medium sauté pan or skillet over high heat, sear veal on one side only until just brown, keeping as rare as possible. Reserve cool.

Lay beef tenderloin flat with cut side up. Rub with the rest of the mustard and garlic and sprinkle with thyme, salt and pepper. Lay veal's browned side down onto center of beef. Fold two long sides of beef into center, enclosing veal. Turn beef over with seam side down. Using butcher's twine loop around beef at 1 to 2 inch intervals. Secure string snugly on the neck using a square knot.

Preheat oven to 450 degrees F.

Season beef with salt, pepper, and mustard. To a large ovenproof skillet or sauté pan, add oil, heat and brown the beef. Remove beef to a warmed plate and deglaze pan by adding wine and scraping stuck bits to loosen. Add shallots, thyme, and bay leaf and reduce by half. Add brown sauce, stir and bring to a simmer. Return beef to the sauce with any plate juices. Put skillet in oven and bake for 20-25 minutes, basting several times. Remove beef to warmed plate. Return skillet with sauce to stovetop, remove bay leaf and reduce by one-third. Add tarragon and butter.

To plate, cut string from beef. Cut beef into 6 slices. Center one slice on warmed plate, surround with sauce and serve.

CRABMEAT BROUSSARD

SERVES 6

Artistry on many levels— appreciate the nuanced subtlety of this historic Creole dish when dining at Broussard's. Brie cream balanced with the full mouth crunch of shrimp en coquille and seasoned bread crumbs, all wrapped in steaming undertones of butter, artichoke, and wine with an insoucent Herbsaint Spinach.

Perfect accompanied by a Vouvray from the Loire Valley and the exquisite tones of Inconspicuous 8. Composed of the leading women university vocal music professors in New Orleans, Inconspicuous 8 provides benefit concerts for local and national charitable causes.

1	Tablespoon butter
6	Jumbo shrimp
2	Tablespoons olive oil
2	Fresh artichoke hearts, chopped
1	Clove garlic, finely chopped
1	Small creole yellow onion, diced
1/4 cup	All purpose flour
1/4 cup	White wine
2	cups Poulet Leek stock [recipe p.202]
1	cup Heavy cream
3	ounces Brie, white rind removed and cubed
1/2 cup	Bread crumbs
3	Tablespoons Whole fresh thyme leaves
3/4 pound	Jumbo lump crabmeat

To make bread crumb mixture, in a small bowl, combine bread crumbs, olive oil and thyme. Reserve.

To make the shrimp, first remove the head, leaving the tail shell intact. Reserve heads for stock. Devein by making a shallow cut atop the tail and removing and discarding the black intestinal tract with the sharp point of a knife or skewer. Butterfly the shrimp by placing sideways and slitting underbelly, inside of curl, to within one-quarter inch of tail. Using hands, open two sides of curl and flatten. In a large skillet or sauté pan over medium heat, melt butter. Sauté shrimp until barely cooked, about 1 minute. Reserve.

To make the brie cream sauce, in a large skillet or sauté pan over medium heat, heat olive oil. Add artichoke hearts, garlic and onion. Sauté until onion is translucent, about 2 minutes. Sprinkle flour into onions, stirring continuously for 1 minute. Deglaze the pan with white wine. Add stock and bring to a boil. Reduce heat and simmer for 3 minutes. Add cream and simmer for 5 minutes. Remove from heat and stand 3 minutes. Add brie, stirring until all brie is melted. Remove from heat and cool. When brie cream sauce has cooled, fold in crabmeat. Do not break crabmeat lumps apart.

Preheat oven to 400 degrees F. In one ovenproof serving dish per serving, center one shrimp so that it stands. Surround shrimp with crabmeat mixture. Sprinkle with breadcrumbs. Repeat for each serving. Place serving dishes on a large baking sheet. Bake until crab is hot and bubbly, about 15 minutes. Serve immediately.

Note: Do not substitute surimi or other imitation crabmeat as it will overwhelm the delicacy of the brie and do not use brie rind in the cream sauce as it will impart an overly strong flavor and texture to the sauce.

CRABMEAT RAVIGOTE

SERVES 6

3   Ears of fresh corn

1/4 cup olive oil

2   Tablespoons Lemon juice

1 1/2 pounds Jumbo lump crabmeat

1   cup Ravigote Sauce, *[recipe p.203]*

18 Endive leaves, white

6   slices, Creole tomato, ripe, cut 1/4 inch thick

12 Shrimp, 10-15 count per pound shrimp, poached

6   Lemon slices

Salt

Parsley

Ravigote is a classic, slightly acidic sauce in creole cuisine. Ravigote means "reinvigorated," certainly the reaction of any creole lady or gentleman dining on this chilled delicacy in the humid New Orleans summer.

Perfect with anything chilled and the cool, smooth tones of Day by Day sung by New Orleans' own jazz great Miss Germaine Bazzle.

Steam corn on cob for 7 to 10 minutes. Remove and allow to cool to room temperature. Cut corn from cob. Marinate corn in olive oil, lemon juice and salt and refrigerate 8 to 12 hours

To make the crabmeat, to a medium bowl, add Ravigote sauce. Fold in crabmeat. Cover and marinate refrigerated 8 to 12 hours.

To plate, place 3 endive leaves meeting in center of plate. Top leaves with 1/4 cup corn. Place 2 slices of tomato on corn. On a slice of tomato, place crabmeat. Top with 2 shrimp and garnish with parsley and lemon.

CRABMEAT TERRINE

Crabmeat Terrine is as complex and elegant as the 5000 pipe Odell Opus 239 Organ commissioned for New Orleans' Trinity Episcopal Church in 1887. Trinity is known for its award winning Trinity Artist Series, as well as the fun and fashionable "Bach Around the Clock" – 29 hours of Bach music, theater, dance and yoga celebrating the Master's birthday on March 21. Celebrate Bach's birthday with this dish.

Perfect accompanied by a crisp white wine while listening to Bach's "Brandenburg Concerto."

To make marinade, in a medium bowl, combine green onion, white, black, and cayenne pepper, salt, lemon juice, white wine, bay leaf and minced garlic.

To make trout, cut trout crosswise into 1-inch pieces. Place trout in marinade and refrigerate for 8 to 12 hours.

To make terrine, in a blender or food processor, combine trout and marinade and purée until very smooth. Add egg whites in three stages, mixing well between additions. Add cream gradually. Transfer to medium bowl and fold in crabmeat, combining thoroughly.

Preheat oven to 325 degrees F. In a 1 to 1-1/2 quart loaf pan, add crabmeat. Place loaf pan in a bain marie or warm water bath consisting of another pan of hot water at least halfway up the side of the loaf pan. bake for 1 1/4 hour at 325 degrees F. When wooden skewer is removed clean, loaf is done. Remove and rest for 15 minutes, unmold and refrigerate. Slice and garnish with crab fingers and fresh parsley.

SERVES 6

1 pound Lake Pontchartrain trout filets
2 Tablespoons Chopped green onions
1/4 teaspoon White pepper
1/4 teaspoon Black pepper
1/4 teaspoon Cayenne pepper
3/4 teaspoons Salt
2 Tablespoons Lemon juice
2 Tablespoons White wine
1 Bay leaf
1/4 teaspoon Minced garlic
1/2 cup Egg whites
1/2 pound Jumbo lump crabmeat
Crab fingers for garnish
Parsley for garnish

CRABMEAT VERSAILLES

SERVES 6

2 Tablespoons butter

1 teaspoon sliced green onions

1 teaspoon minced dry shallots

1/4 teaspoon minced garlic

1/2 cup white wine

1/4 lemon, juiced

1 3/4 cups Béchamel Sauce,
    medium thick *[recipe p.194]*

1 Tablespoon fresh dill

1 1/2 pounds jumbo lump crabmeat

1/2 cup freshly grated Parmigiano-
    Reggiano

Salt

Pinch Broussard's House Made
    Creole Seasonings *[recipe p.196]*

3 lemons, halved

6 fresh dill sprigs

Continental cuisine is the true test of a chef's classical training. Gunter and Evelyn Preusses' Versailles Restaurant was the unquestioned leader of Continental cuisine in the City.

Enjoy with a French white Vouvray while listening to Louisiana Philharmonic Orchestra harpist Rachel Van Voorhees' release "Bring a Torch Jeanette Isabella."

To make the crabmeat, in a large skillet or sauté pan over medium heat, melt butter.

Sauté green onions, shallots, and garlic without browning, about 2 minutes.

Add wine and lemon juice and reduce by half. Add Béchamel Sauce and dill and reduce by one-third. Add lump crabmeat, season to taste with salt and cayenne pepper and simmer for ten minutes.

To plate, into six ramekins or small seashells, spoon the crabmeat, sprinkle with Parmigiano-Reggiano and bake until cheese is golden and sauce is bubbly, about five minutes. Garnish with dill sprig and half lemon.

OYSTERS BIENVILLE

Jean Baptiste Le Moyne, Sieur de Bienville was appointed Governor of French Louisiana on four different occasions from 1701 - 1743. In 1720, Bienville ordered plans for a new city, a seven block rectangle, now known as the French Quarter. The original map is in the Library of Congress and indicates that Broussard's location, now called Square 70, Lot 384 was built and fenced in 1722 and owned by the Surgeon for the French Crown colony.

Enjoy this Broussard's spin on an old classic with a Gewürztraminer from Alsace and Beethoven's busy, cheerful 6th!

To clarify margarine, in a large skillet or sauté pan over low heat, melt margarine. When totally melted, remove from heat and stand. Solids will fall to the bottom and oil will float to the top. Skim oil and use as clarified margarine.

In a large saucepan over medium high heat, melt butter and sauté onion, bell pepper, and mushrooms until bell pepper is limp. Add Tasso, garlic, paprika, basil, and cayenne, sautéing for another 5 minutes. Add flour and sauté for 2 minutes. Reduce heat to medium and whisk in cream, Half & Half, worcestershire, and hot sauce. Season to taste with salt. Add shrimp and simmer, reducing until thick enough to mound on a spoon. Adjust seasonings if needed. If making ahead, refrigerate and reserve chilled.

Preheat oven to 325 degrees F.

On a baking sheet, place oyster shell without oyster. Fill shell with Tasso shrimp mixture. Bake until topping is brown and bubbly, about 20 minutes. While mixture is baking, make fried oysters by putting Panko crumbs in one 11 x 7 x 2-inch baking pan and eggs in another 11 x 7 x 2-inch baking pan. In a large skillet or sauté pan over medium heat, warm clarified margarine. Keep skillet warm. Dip oysters in eggs and then in Panko breadcrumbs. Shake off the excess flour. Quickly place in warmed skillet or sauté pan. Sauté until edges begins to brown, turning once.

To plate, place six oysters shells on plate, top with fried oyster and drizzle with melted butter. Garnish with parsley and serve immediately.

SERVES 6

1/2 pound Tasso, finely chopped

1/2 stick Butter

3/4 cup Diced creole yellow onion

1/3 cup Diced green bell pepper

1/3 cup Diced red bell pepper

1/2 cup Sliced fresh mushrooms

1 small Clove garlic, minced

1/2 teaspoon Paprika

1 teaspoon Minced fresh basil leaves

1/2 teaspoon Cayenne

1/2 cup All-purpose flour

1 cup Heavy cream

1 cup Half & half

1 teaspoon Worcestershire sauce

1/2 teaspoon Louisiana style hot sauce

1 1/2 pounds 70-90 count Shrimp, peeled

36 Raw oysters, shucked

36 Oyster shells

1 cup Margarine

5 Eggs, beaten

Panko breadcrumbs

Salt

OYSTERS LAFITTE WITH CRAWFISH BECHAMÉL

SERVES 6

2   Tablespoons Butter

2   Tablespoons Sliced green onions

1   Tablespoon Minced French shallots

1   teaspoon Minced garlic

1/2 cup White wine

1   Lemon, juiced

1 3/4 cups Bechamél Sauce *[recipe p.194]*

1 1/2 Tablespoons Fresh dill

1 1/2 pounds Boiled crawfish tail meat

Salt

Pinch cayenne

18 Large raw oysters on the half-shell

1/4 cup Parmigiano-Reggiano

6   Whole boiled crawfish

Lafitte —a name of much confusion and many meanings. Jean Lafitte is the sometimes merchant, sometimes privateer, sometimes pirate without whom General Andrew Jackson would not have won the Battle of New Orleans. Pardoned by Governor William C.C. Claiborne and then pursued again. Born in Santo Domingo or Paulliac, France? Died in Cartagena or Galveston? Buried where no one knows. "Lafitte" is also the fishing village on Bayou Barataria that bears his name and, some say, is inhabited by the descendants of the privateer's sailors, the Baratarians. Jean Lafitte National Historic Park and Preserve is composed of 6 locations scattered about the State, appropriate for a man who roamed the entire State at will, leaving an elusive trail of legend and myth behind. So will this dish linger in your memory.

Indulge your inner privateer with a Pinot Blanc while listening to the hauntingly beautiful theme song composed by Elmer Bernstein for the 1958 movie classic "The Buccaneer" staring Yul Brynner as Jean Lafitte, filmed partially in New Orleans.

Preheat oven to 350 degrees F.

To make Crawfish Bechamél, in a medium saucepan over medium heat, sauté onions, shallots and garlic until soft but not browned, about 2 minutes. Add white wine and lemon juice and reduce by half. Add Bechamél sauce and dill and reduce by a third. Add crawfish tails and simmer for 10 minutes. Salt to taste. Add cayenne.

Cover the bottom of an 11-by-17 baking sheet, with rock salt. Place oyster shells with raw oysters on rock salt. Spoon Crawfish Bechamél atop raw oyster and sprinkle with Parmigiano-Reggiano. Bake until cheese is golden and sauce is bubbling.

To plate each serving, place three oysters per plate. Garnish with one whole boiled crawfish.

OYSTERS BROUSSARD

Long one of the top honeymoon destinations in America, it is no wonder New Orleans has rapidly become one of the top destination wedding locations as well. Many wedding receptions at Broussard's include this incredible appetizer.

On your wedding day, it is best enjoyed with a Sancerre, made from the Sauvignon blanc grape grown in the Loire valley, while listening to the sound of your love's laughter!

In a large skillet or sauté pan over medium high heat, melt butter. Add onion and bell peppers and sauté for 5 minutes. Add zucchini, eggplant, and mushrooms, continue sautéing until zucchini is softened but not of purée consistency, about another 5 minutes. Add flour, mix well over medium high heat for 1 minute. Deglaze the pan by adding wine and scraping cooked, particles. Add tomato purée, sugar, oregano, Worcestershire sauce, Louisiana-style Hot Sauce, salt and pepper to taste and mix well. Add bay leaf and reduce heat to simmer. Simmer until thick, about 30 minutes. Test mixture, by mounding on a spoon. Remove bay leaves. Refrigerate and reserve chilled.

Preheat oven to 325 degrees F.

On a baking sheet, place oyster shell with raw oyster in shell. Spoon vegetable sauté atop each raw oyster. Bake until topping is brown and bubbly, about 20 minutes. Serve immediately, plating 6 oysters per serving.

SERVES 6

- 1 stick Butter, unsalted
- 1/2 pound Creole yellow onions, diced
- 1/2 pound Red bell peppers, seeded and diced
- 1/2 pound Green bell peppers, seeded and diced
- 1 pound Zucchini, sliced
- 1 pound Eggplant, skinned and diced
- 1 pound Fresh mushrooms, sliced
- 1/2 cup All-purpose flour
- 1 cup White wine
- 2 quarts Tomato purée
- 1 pound Sugar
- 1 1/2 teaspoons Oregano, dried
- 1 1/2 teaspoons Worcestershire sauce
- 1/4 teaspoon Louisiana-style Hot Sauce
- 1 teaspoon White pepper
- 6 Bay leaves
- 36 Oysters on the half-shell
- Salt

OYSTERS ROCKEFELLER

SERVES 6

2 Strips bacon, minced

1/2 pound Celery ribs, minced

1 handful Parsley, minced

1/2 cup Chopped creole yellow
   onion

1 small Clove garlic, minced

Pinch ground nutmeg

1 pound Spinach, finely chopped

1/2 cup All-purpose flour

1 Tablespoon Herbsaint

1/2 cup Heavy cream

1 teaspoon Worcestershire sauce

Salt

1/2 teaspoon White pepper

36 Oysters on the half-shall

1/2 cup grated Parmigiano-Reggiano

Of the four Grande Dame Restaurants of Creole Cuisine, each is known for its own distinctive oyster appetizer. Here Broussard's builds upon Antoine's Oysters Rockefeller, adding a Broussard's twist. While Antoine's exact recipe remains a secret, spinach is often cited as an ingredient in variations. Feel free, however, to substitute the traditional Gombo Zhebes combination of spinach, turnip, and mustard greens, beet tops, lettuce, green cabbage, green celery leaves and green onion tops for a rich experience.

Enjoy with a Monrachet from Burgundy while listening to — what else but the lyric "If I ever had a dime, I would be rich, rich as Rockefeller" from the song On The Sunny Side of the Street sung by Louis Armstrong!

In a large saucepan over medium-high heat, sauté bacon until crisp. Add celery, parsley, onion, garlic, and nutmeg, sautéing for 4 minutes. Add spinach, continuing to sauté for another 8 minutes. Add flour and sauté for 1 minute.

Over high heat, add Herbsaint, deglazing the pan by loosening and scraping the well cooked bits. Whisk in cream, Worcestershire sauce, salt and pepper, bringing to a boil and reducing until can mound on a spoon. Remove from heat and transfer to a blender or food processor and purée. Refrigerate and reserve chilled.

Preheat oven to 325 degrees F.

On a baking sheet, put oyster shell with raw oyster in shell. Spoon purée atop each raw oyster. Sprinkle with Parmigiano-Reggiano. Bake until topping is brown and bubbly, about 20 minutes. Serve immediately, plating 6 oysters per serving.

SHRIMP MARQUIS DE LAFAYETTE

SERVES 6

1 1/2 dozen 10 - 15 count Shrimp

Salt

Black Pepper

2   cups Louisiana Crabcake, prior to
    frying [recipe p.132]

Oil

1 1/4 cups Creole-Mustard Caper
    Sauce [recipe p.199]

Just when one thinks one has experienced without question the richest, most complex dishes imaginable, Lafayette appears! Rich, complex, gentile and with as much integrity as the Marquis himself.

Enjoy with a Chablis while listening to *Lift Every Voice for Freedom* arranged by New Orleans own Moses Hogan commissioned by the Spokane Festival of the Arts in honor of the victims of the September 11, 2001 attack on the United States and performed by the Moses Hogan Choral Singers.

Peel and devein shrimp, leaving ends of tails. Butterfly shrimp with a deep cut and stand in baking pan. Salt and pepper to taste. Divide crabcake mixture into 18 portions and ball.

Preheat oven to 400 degrees.

Place a ball on each shrimp. Fold tail of shrimp over top to cover crabcake. Place shrimp in well-oiled baking pan. Bake for 5 minutes.

To plate, removed shrimp from oven and place 3 shrimp on each serving plate. Spoon Creole Mustard-Caper Sauce beside each shrimp. Serve immediately.

THE JOSEPHINE ROOM

Josephine Bonaparte was a Creole! She was born Marie Josèphe Rose Tascher de La Pagerie in Martinique to a Creole family who owned a sugar plantation. Often called Rose Tasher informally, she went by the name Rose until she married Napoleon who asked her to use Josèphe.

The dining room named in her honor was part of the Hermann-Grima complex and is believed to date to 1834. Many theories have been advanced as to its original use — as a single animal stable, a kitchen, a washroom, but none have been confirmed.

The Josephine room is decorated in the rustic French provençal style with wide planked flooring, pegged instead of nailed, and rugged beams. Wainscoting mimics the wainscoting used in Provençe as thermal insulation on stone walls. In keeping with an authentic style, many multi-paneled doors and windows are used to maximize natural light and open to the courtyard. Traditional provençal chandeliers were simply made with large curved metal fittings. The provençal chandeliers in the Josephine room also exhibit hand painted color. The original wallpaper was a green Fortuny toile depicting French country scenes designed by Mariano Fortuny of Palazzo Orfei in Venice. The wallpaper has been replaced twice since its major renovation. The most well-known piece of provençal furniture is the armoire. An antique walnut armoire imported from Provençe by Charles Gresham is centered in the Josephine room. On the pegged boiserie door of the armoire is a hand carved sunflower, a symbol of Provençe. Sconces flanking the doorway exhibit the fleur de lis, a symbol both of Bourbon France and New Orleans and just outside the Josephine room, waiting in the courtyard, is a beautifully placed gas light — an invitation to the courtyard.

In the Josephine Room...

...Mother's Day

LOUISIANA BOUILLABAISSE

MAKES 1 GALLON

BROTH

1 cup Hot water

1/8 ounce Saffron

1/2 pound Carrots, cut lengthwise and diagonally sliced

1/2 pound Celery, cut lengthwise and diagonally sliced

1/2 pound Onions, diced

1/2 pound Fennel, cut lengthwise and diagonally sliced

1/2 pound Green peppers, diced

1/2 cup Olive oil

1 Tablespoon Minced garlic

1/4 cup Diced shallots

1/2 cup Tomato paste

1 gallon Shrimp or fish stock, warmed

2 cups Chopped tomatoes

3 Bay leaves

Salt

White pepper

SEAFOOD

1 pound Raw shrimp, peeled and deveined

1 cup Raw oysters without shells

1/2 pound Lump crabmeat

1/2 pound Peeled crawfish tail meat

1/2 pound Fresh fish filet, gutted, scaled, deboned and 1-inch dice

1/2 pound Raw scallops

18 Fresh mussels

Basil

A Creole version of a French classic, using the freshest of Louisiana ingredients makes even Escoffier jealous!

Sip ae French white Montrachet while listening to Louisiana three time Grammy Award nominee David Greely's version of Lune de Miel [Honeymoon Waltz] from his release, "Sud du Sud."

To make broth, in a one cup oven-safe measuring cup, pour boiling water. Put saffron in boiling water to bloom.

In a large stockpot over medium-high heat, warm olive oil. Add carrots, celery and fennel and sauté until partially cooked, about 3 minutes. Add onions, peppers, garlic, shallots, and stir in tomato paste, cooking for 10 minutes, stirring constantly. Add warmed stock. Add tomatoes, saffron in water, salt, pepper, and bay leaves. Bring to a full boil, remove from heat, cool and refrigerate or freeze.

To assemble soup, in a large stockpot, bring 6 cups of broth to a boil and reduce heat to simmer. Add mussels, fish oysters, crawfish, crabmeat, and shrimp and simmer until shrimp are pink, 3 to 5 minutes. Pour broth into large soup plate. Arrange 3 mussels one-third each around the plate starting in the 12 o'clock position. Arrange rest of seafood in a similar one-third manner. Serve immediately.

Note: Broussard's Bouillabaisse Creole Stew Base is also available as a frozen item through New Orleans Fish House at www.NewOrleansFishHouse.com.

POMPANO AND SCALLOPS NAPOLEON WITH CREOLE MUSTARD-CAPER SAUCE

Joseph Broussard, part Cajun and part Creole, loved Napoleon, a favorite with New Orleans Creoles. In the 1800s, folktales abounded that Napoleon secretly escaped and lived in disguise in Louisiana, alas, all the products of wishful thinking. Napoleon was a man of the people and an energetic, fearless General like Broussard's own legendary ancestor, the Acadian military leader Joseph Broussard dit "Beausoleil". No wonder Joseph Broussard named his beautiful patio for the French military genius.

Enjoy this dish at Broussard's with a French white wine while listening to Billy Holiday's version of Do You Know What It Means to Miss New Orleans from her only major film "New Orleans."

Pound pompano gently with the flat of a large cleaver. Sprinkle with Broussard's House Made Creole Seasonings Mix. Grill or broil fish and shrimp until no longer translucent and scallop edges are just brown.

Place Creole Mustard-Caper Sauce on plate. Remove toothpick and place cooked pompano and scallop and shrimp on plate on top of the Creole Mustard-Caper Sauce. Garnish with baby green onion and red bell pepper.

MAKES 1 GALLON

- 6   6-ounce Pompano fillets, cut in half lengthwise
- 12 Large scallops, cleaned
- 12 10-15 count shrimp, raw, shelled with tail on
- 1 1/4 cups Creole Mustard-Caper Sauce [recipe p.199]
- 6   Tablespoons Broussard's House Made Creole Seasonings [recipe p.196]
- 6   Green onion spears as garnish
- 6   Red pepper sticks as garnish

WILD SALMON WITH LEMON BUTTER PECAN STUFFING

SERVES 6

6   5-ounce Wild salmon fillets

4   cups Fine bread crumbs

4   cups Pecan pieces

2   cups Chopped parsley

2   cups Chopped green onions

1/2 cup Lemon zest

1   cup Lemon juice

4   cups Softened butter

Salt

Black pepper

Cayenne pepper

In 1803, financed through the Louisiana Purchase, President Thomas Jefferson commissioned the Corp of Discovery, led by U.S. Army Captain Meriwether Lewis and William Clark, a retired Army officer chosen by Lewis. Exploring the Louisiana Purchase territory led by a fifteen year old female Shoshone guide name Sacajawea, on August 13, 1805, Lewis wrote, "An Indian gave me a piece of fresh salmon roasted, which I ate with a very good relish." On January 4, 1806, he noted that "...the natives of the Columbia...annually prepare about 30,000 pounds of pounded sammon..."

Like a canoe over a rapid, this bustling, expressive and exuberant dish is best enjoyed with a Chardonny from Napa and the equally exuberant Grammy Award winning recording by Louisiana Philharmonic Orchestra's own Carlos Miguel Prieto of Korngold's "Violin Concerto in D major, Op. 35."

Cut a pocket for stuffing in the salmon filets by cutting halfway through the depth of the fillets lengthwise. From the middle cut crosswise half the depth of the fillets to form a pocket. Cover and reserve.

Preheat oven to 350 degrees F.

In a medium mixing bowl, combine bread crumbs, pecan pieces, parsley, green onions, lemon zest and lemon juice. Fold in the softened butter and season to taste with salt, black pepper and cayenne pepper. Stuff mixture into pockets in fillets. Place stuffed fillets in a buttered baking pan and roast in preheated oven until salmon is cooked, about 10 minutes.

REDFISH WITH CRAB IN LEMON HERBSAINT CREAM

Avid fishermen consider Louisiana one of the best places in the world for top redfish action. Inland waterways and coastal marshes provide such a perfect habitat for these plentiful big beauties that "double catches" on the same hook are not unusual.

Serve with a French Bordeaux from Margaux while listening to Jelly Roll Morton and His Red Hot Peppers version of Joseph "King" Oliver and Walter Melrose's stomp *Dr. Jazz*.

In a large, sauté pan or skillet over medium heat, combine Herbsaint, wine, shallots, carrots, celery, leeks, and mushrooms. Bring to a simmer. Add redfish and poach until flesh is firm but not dry, about 8-10 minutes. Remove fish to warmed plate and reserve warm.

Increase heat to high and reduce poaching liquid by half. Lower heat to medium. Add room temperature cream and reduce by half again. Season with salt and pepper to taste and lemon juice. Reduce to a simmer and add crabmeat, tossing until thoroughly heated. Finish by swirling in the butter and splashing with Herbsaint. Place a bed of 1/4 cup of rice pilaf on plate. Top rice with fish. Spoon sauce over warm fish, garnish with a sprig of dill and a lemon curl and serve immediately.

Note: Bass may be substituted for Redfish.

SERVES 6

1/2 cup Herbsaint liquor

3/4 cup white wine

1 Tablespoon finely chopped shallots

1/4 cup julienned carrots

1/4 cup julienned celery

1/4 cup julienned leeks, white only

6 fresh mushroom caps, stems removed and sliced

6 4-ounce redfish fillets

1 1/2 cups heavy cream, room temperature

6 Tablespoons butter, unsalted

3 lemons, juiced

3/4 pound lump crabmat

1 1/2 sticks butter

Splash of Herbsaint

1 1/2 cups Rice with Tasso, reserved warm *[recipe p.204]*

Dill and lemon peel as garnish

Salt

White pepper

TROUT CHOPIN

SERVES 6

1/2 cup Chopped green onions

2 Tablespoons Dry shallots

1 small Clove garlic, chopped

2 dozen 21-25 count, Raw peeled shrimp

1 Tablespoon Chopped fresh dill

1/4 cup Dry vermouth

6 5-6 ounce Trout fillets, skinned

1 cup Heavy cream

6 Tablespoons Butter, unsalted

1/2 teaspoon Lemon juice

Salt

White pepper

Kate O'Flaherty of St. Louis Missouri married Oscar Chopin, the son of Victor Jean Baptiste Chopin and Julia Benoist Chopin of Clouthierville and New Orleans and in 1870. She moved to the French Quarter where Oscar worked in the Cotton Exchange. Her experiences here led to her ground breaking novel The Awakening set in New Orleans and Grand Isle. Kate Chopin walked before 819 Conti, which was already about 40 years old when Kate lived here.

Enjoy with Broussard's "Delicato" Chardonnay while listening to Kate's original composition for piano *Lilia's Polka* published in 1888.

Preheat oven to 350 degrees F.

In a large, cold sauté pan or skillet, combine green onions, shallots, garlic, shrimp, mushrooms, dill and vermouth. Warm skillet over low heat. Lay trout fillets atop a bed of vegetables and completely cover the top of the trout with other vegetables from the skillet. Cover skillet with foil and roast in oven until trout is just cooked, about 10 minutes. Remove trout and shrimp from skillet and reserve warm. Return skillet to stove top and over high heat, reduce liquids by half. Lower heat and add cream, butter, salt and pepper to taste. While stirring continuously, add lemon juice and incorporate fully. Simmer for 5 minutes. Place trout on warmed plate and top with shrimp. Spoon vegetables atop shrimp and trout and serve immediately.

SALMON DE LA SALLE

René-Robert Cavelier, Sieur de La Salle, faced a conundrum early in his adulthood, whether to continue as a Jesuit priest or to become an explorer. He left the order and on April 9, 1682, buried an engraved plate and a cross in what is today Venice, Louisiana, claiming all lands drained by the Mississippi River for France and naming them La Louisiane.

Sample a vintage white wine from Napa while listening to Sasha Masakowski & Musical Playground's version of "Wishes," another hidden treasure.

In a blender or food processor, combine tomatoes, bell peppers, onions, garlic, lemon juice and parsley. Add olive oil and lemon and stir.

In a large, cold sauté pan or skillet, combine green onions, shallots, garlic, shrimp, mushrooms, dill and vermouth. Warm skillet over low heat. Lay salmon fillets atop bed of vegetables and completely cover the top of the salmon, hiding it with other vegetables from the skillet. Cover skillet with foil and roast in oven until salmon is just cooked, about 10 minutes. Remove salmon and shrimp from skillet and reserve warm. Return skillet to stove top and over high heat, reduce liquids by half. Lower heat and add cream, butter, salt and pepper to taste. While stirring continuously, add lemon juice and incorporate fully. Simmer for 5 minutes. Place salmon on warmed plate and top with vegetables. Garnish with lemon and parsley and serve immediately.

SERVES 6

2 dozen Plum tomatoes, skinned

3 green Bell peppers, seeded and roughly chopped

2 medium Creole yellow onions, rough chopped

1 small Clove garlic

2 cups Tomato juice

1 Tablespoon chopped fresh parsley

1 cup Olive oil

4 Lemons, juiced

Salt

White pepper

Louisiana Hot Sauce

Cumin

1/2 cup Tablespoon Corn oil

2 dozen 1-ounce Salmon fillet slices

1 1/2 dozen Thin lemon slices

Parsley Sprigs

STUFFED EGGPLANT BAYOU TECHE

WITH BROUSSARD'S ORIGINAL WARM REMOULADE

The American Culinary Federation is the largest professional chefs association in North America. ACF Culinary Team USA, a program of the American Culinary Federation (ACF), is the official representative team of the United States in major national and international culinary competitions, the "Olympic Team" of the culinary world. Broussard's Gunter Preuss was the team leader. This dish was created for the Pan-American Culinary Olympics held in New Orleans.

Wonderful with a Pinot Noir from New Zealand and the exquisite Leah Chase's version of Love Me Again.

To make crabmeat stuffing, in a skillet or sauté pan over medium heat, melt butter. Add green and yellow onions, sautéing until softened. Add cream and white wine and bring to a boil. Reduce heat and simmer until liquids somewhat reduced and start to thicken, about 2 to 3 minutes. Fold in bread crumbs and lemon juice. Simmer until forms a mass capable of shaping. Fold in crabmeat. Season to taste with salt and pepper and reserve hot.

To make eggplant, lightly sprinkle eggplant rounds and shrimp with salt, black pepper, cayenne, and paprika. Dredge eggplant and shrimp in white flour and dip in egg wash. Roll eggplant in bread crumbs and shrimp in yellow corn meal. Deep fry shrimp and eggplant.

To plate, place one slice of eggplant on a heated serving plate and spoon hot crabmeat stuffing atop. Top with one fried shrimp. Top with second eggplant slice and second shrimp. Finish with green onion top. Spoon Warm Remoulade Sauce on top.

SERVES 6

2 cups Crabmeat Stuffing, recipe below

12 Eggplant rounds, 1 1/2 inches thick

1 dozen 10-15 count Shrimp

1 cup Flour

Egg wash of 1 whole egg and 1/4 cup of milk

Bread crumbs for rolling

1 cup Yellow corn flour

6 Green onion tops, 3 inches long

1 1/2 cups Warm Remoulade Sauce *[recipe p.209]*

Salt

Black pepper

Cayenne pepper

Paprika

CRABMEAT STUFFING

1/2 cup Butter

1 bunch Green onions, chopped

1 small Creole yellow onion, chopped

1 cup Heavy cream

1/2 cup White wine

1 cup Bread crumbs

1/4 cup Lemon juice

1/2 pound White crabmeat

Salt

White pepper

TROUT MARCUS PREUSS

SERVES 6

1 cup Margarine

5 Eggs, beaten

All-purpose flour

6 Six-ounce trout fillets

Salt

White pepper

1/2 teaspoon Lemon juice

3/4 cup Clarified margarine

Marcus Sauce

2 Tablespoons Chopped parsley

MARCUS SAUCE

6 Fresh, trimmed and cooked
   artichoke bottoms

2 Tablespoon Sliced green onions

1/2 teaspoons Chopped dry shallots

1/2 teaspoon Chopped garlic

1/4 cup sliced Portobello
   mushrooms

1/2 cup White wine

1/2 cup Lemon juice

1 cup Fresh butter, divided into
   thirds

Salt

White pepper

Dill

Carrots

This dish was named by Chef Gunter Preuss to honor his son, the General Manager of Broussard's, Marcus "Marc" Preuss, who is both a devoted son and a dedicated restaurateur, carrying on his family's legacy. Without Marc, there would be no next generation of Broussard's in the Preuss family.

Delicious with two of Marc's favorites at Broussard's, a Sauvignon Blanc from New Zealand and Kid Merv's Body & Soul.

To clarify margarine, in a large skillet or sauté pan over low heat, melt margarine. When totally melted, remove from heat and stand. Solids will fall to the bottom and oil will float to the top. Skim oil and use as clarified margarine.

To make trout, put flour in one 11 x 7 x 2-inch baking pan and eggs in another 11 x 7 x 2-inch baking pan.

In a large skillet or sauté pan over medium heat, warm clarified margarine. Keep skillet warm while flouring trout.

Season fillets with salt, pepper, and lemon juice. Dip fillet into beaten eggs and dredge in flour. Shake off excess flour and quickly place in skillet or sauté pan. Sauté until edges begin to brown, turn, and cook until flakes easily, about 5 minutes.

To make Marcus sauce, in a medium skillet or sauté pan, combine artichoke bottoms, onions, shallots, garlic, mushrooms, wine, and lemon juice. Bring to a boil. Add 3 pieces of butter at once so melts evenly and swirl pan

To plate, place in center of warmed plate. Spoon Marcus sauce atop and around trout. Garnish with dill and carrots.

Note: Both butter and margarine contain 80% fat. While clarified butter is most often seen in recipes, margarine may also be clarified and is sometimes preferred for preparations such as the pan frying in this recipe. Keep separated butter or margarine solids refrigerated and use them as a final finish in any dish requiring richness or heavy cream.

LOUISIANA PECAN CRUSTED DRUM

Whether you say PEA-CAN or PAH-COWN, local Native Americans said "pacane" meaning "nut to be cracked by rock." Pecan trees have grown wild here since pre-historic times. The first known shipment of pecans from Louisiana was a box of "pacan nuts" from Daniel Clark, United States Consul to New Orleans, sent to Thomas Jefferson on March 12, 1779. Thomas Jefferson added pecans to his garden at Monticello and in 1794 gave his friend George Washington saplings which were planted at Mount Vernon. Pecans grow today in Washington's experimental "little garden" at Mount Vernon.

Enjoy with a Pinot Noir while listening to "Satchmo of the Ghetto" trumpeter James Andrews' Night Life from his release The Big Time Stuff.

Mix together pecans and panko and reserve.

Season fish with salt and pepper on both sides. Place fish in buttermilk for 5 minutes. Remove and place in pecans and panko mix. To a large sauce pan add butter and oil and bring to medium heat. Add drum, cooking until a golden brown crust forms, about 4 minutes per side.

To plate, place small amount of Tamari-style soy beurre blanc sauce on plate, top with pecan crusted drum. Top drum with Tamari-style beurre blanc, making sure to place an adequate amount of crawfish atop the fish. Garnish with grilled half lemon, sprig of dill and a whole boiled crawfish.

SERVES 6

6 4-5 ounce Drum fillets, skinned and boned

1 cup Pecans, finely chopped

1 cup Panko bread crumbs

1 quart Buttermilk

3 Tablespoons unsalted Butter

3 Tablespoons Salad oil

3 cups Tamari-style Soy Beurre Blanc *[recipe p.208]*

Grilled half of lemon

Whole boiled crawfish

Dill

Salt

White pepper

SALMON JEAN LAFITTE

SERVES 6

1/2 cup Herbsaint liquor

3/4 cup White wine

1 Tablespoon Finely chopped
  Shallots

1/4 cup julienned Celery

1/4 cup julienned Leeks, white only

6 fresh Mushroom caps, stems
  removed and sliced

6 4-ounce Salmon fillets

1 1/2 cups Heavy cream, room
  temperature

6 Tablespoons Butter, unsalted

Salt

White pepper

3 Lemons, juiced

3/4 pound Lump crabmeat

1 1/2 sticks Butter

Splash of Herbsaint

1 1/2 cups Rice with Tasso,
  reserved warm [Recipe in
  Kitchen Section]

Spinach, red pepper, dill and
  lemon peel as garnish

Lafitte is not only the name of a famous privateer. The fishing village of Lafitte, located just south of New Orleans in the Barataria Basin, is surrounded by marshland. Lafitte hosts marinas, fishing guides, swamp tours, bed and breakfasts, the annual Blessing of the Fleet and when the marshland erupts in thousands of blooms, Lafitte's Iris Festival.

Savor a Côte du Rhône while listening to third generation musician Brandon Foret's recording of Gravity with the Brandon Foret Band.

In a large, sauté pan or skillet over medium heat, combine Herbsaint, wine, shallots, celery, leeks, and mushrooms. Bring to a simmer. Add salmon and poach until flesh is firm but not dry, about 8-10 minutes. Remove fish to warmed plate and reserve warm.

Increase heat to high and reduce poaching liquid by half. Lower heat to medium. Add room temperature cream and reduce by half again. Season with salt and pepper to taste and lemon juice. Reduce to a simmer and add crabmeat, tossing until thoroughly heated. Finish by swirling in the butter and splashing with Herbsaint. Place a bed of 1/4 cup of rice pilaf on plate. Top rice with fish. Spoon sauce over warm fish, garnish with spinach, red pepper, a sprig of dill and a lemon slice and serve immediately.

THE COURTYARD

The singularly most important feature of a French Quarter Creole abode is the courtyard. For Broussard's courtyard, no effort was spared. The giant antique flagstone slabs were lifted. The slabs were originally used as ballast in ships entering the port of New Orleans. As the ships took on cargo, they unloaded the ballast and thrifty New Orleans covered their mud courtyards with them to make a useable surface. Similar slabs, can be found throughout the French Quarter.

A massive drainage system was installed. French Quarter lots were all graded higher at the back and lower in the front to promote drainage through the carriageway and onto the street. As a result, water would flood the main dining room in hard rains. The team raised the dining room 3 feet and placed an extensive drainage system under it. Additional drain pipes were placed under the Josephine room, diverting the water into a side parking lot and then to the street. A drain system of iron grates was placed in the patio proper. The original flagstones were leveled and replaced and additional antique slabs were purchased. A brick walkway was added next to the Magnolia Room using purchased and reclaimed antique brick. Raised planting beds and a fountain were added.

The Wisteria plant in the courtyard is the oldest in the French Quarter, already well established when Joseph Broussard married his Rosalie. During the renovation, it was protected from construction damage. A steel arbor was built to accommodate the wisteria. Plans were drawn for the structure in order to allow the wisteria to move and grow. The wisteria blooms twice in the Spring, drawing a crowd of admirers.

In the Courtyard...

...Wisteria

DUCK RILLETTES

A duck hunter's dream, New Orleans is virtually surrounded by some of the best waterfowl habitat in the world, including the Pearl River, Manchac, Joyce, Maurepas Swamp, Biloxi, Salvadore/Timken/Couba Island, and Pass-A-Loutre Wildlife Management Areas and the Bogue Chitto, Big Branch, and Delta National Wildlife Refuges.

Delicious with a Spanish red wine while listening to the "décimas" folk songs in the Islenos language, some dating back to the middle ages, sung by the late Irvan Perez, a 1991 winner of the National Endowment for the Arts National Heritage Fellowship, from St. Bernard parish, who performed at the Wolf Trap National Folk Festival and the New Orleans Jazz and Heritage Festival and for King Juan Carlos I and Queen Sofia of Spain. Irvan Perez was also an expert carver of duck decoys. His decoys have been exhibited at the Smithsonian.

MAKES 2 1/2 POUNDS

One 6 pound duckling, quartered

1/3 bottle dry white wine

1 creole yellow onion, sliced

1 clove garlic, finely chopped

4 sprigs fresh thyme

1 cup clarified butter

1 loaf French bread

Salt

Freshly ground black pepper

Preheat the oven to 400 degrees F.

To make the fillets, brown duckling quarters, turning often, until fat begins to render, about 30 minutes.

Add wine, onion, garlic and thyme and roast until duck is done, about 20 minutes per pound Cool to room temperature.

Drain jus and fat from pan, reserving liquids.

When cool, shred duck meat and skin, discarding bones. Added shredded duck to jus and mix. Season with salt to taste. Season liberally with pepper.

Chill rillette and spoon into small crock. Seal top of crock with clarified butter and refrigerate. Serve cold with French bread.

MARINATED PORK TENDERLOIN

WITH APPLES, CELERY, AND LOUISIANA SWEET POTATO HASHBROWNS

Broussard's slow roasted marinated pork is simply delicious in its complexity of tastes!

This dish cries out for a saucy Cabernet Sauvignon from Sonoma while listening to Sarah Savoy and the Francadian's song "Leve tes fenêtres haute" from their release "C'est Savoy." While a musical powerhouse in her own right, Sarah is also the daughter of two Louisiana music legends -- Marc Savoy and Ann Savoy.

In a medium mixing bowl, combine all marinade ingredients. In a glass baking dish, pour in half of the marinade, put pork filets atop marinade, pour rest of marinade atop pork. Cover and refrigerate for 24 hours. Turn filets several times while marinating.
Preheat oven to 400 degrees F.

Heat a covered skillet until very hot. Add oil to skillet. Place filets in skillet and brown on both sides. Remove filets to plate and drain excess oil from skillet. Add wine, mustard, shallots, butter and garlic to skillet. Stir well to dissolve mustard. Add Brown Sauce, vinegar, hot sauce and mix well. Return the pork filets to skillet with any juices on the plate. Place in oven until cooked medium, about 8-10 minutes. Remove filets and reserve warm. Return skillet to stovetop. Add butter to sauce in skillet and season to taste with salt and pepper.

To plate, place sautéed celery in upper right quarter of warmed plate. Shingle apple wedges in the upper left quarter next to the celery. Prop hash browns on celery on right side of the plate. Cut and fan pork filet into 4 slices. Rest first 2 slices of fan on apple wedges. Spoon sauce onto left side of plate and over pork. Garnish with thyme sprig.

SERVES 6

MARINADE

6   Tablespoons sliced Carrots

4   Tablespoons sliced Onions

2   Tablespoons sliced Celery

1   cup Soy sauce

2/3 cup White wine

1/2 cup Salad oil

4   cloves bruised Garlic

5   sprigs fresh Thyme

6   6-ounce Pork tenderloin filets

SAUCE

6   Tablespoons Vegetable oil

1   cup White wine

1 1/2 Tablespoons Dijon-style mustard

1   teaspoon chopped Shallots

2   Tablespoons fresh Butter

1   teaspoon chopped Garlic

1   cup Brown Sauce #2 [recipe p.196]

1   teaspoon white Vinegar

Dash Louisiana-style hot sauce

SALT

White pepper

2   Tablespoons Butter

Sautéed Apples [recipe p.206]

Sautéed Celery Julienne [recipe p.206]

Sweet Potato Hash Browns [recipe p.208]

6   prigs fresh Thyme

ANCHO-CARAWAY RUBBED PORK CHOP

6   10-ounce Pork chops

3   cups Ancho-Caraway Rub
    [recipe p.193]

2   1/4 cups Molasses Mustard
    Horseradish Sauce [recipe p.201]

Parsley, freshly chopped

Salt

Black pepper

Ancho Chile powder is made from dried Poblano peppers and is available in specialty shops.

Delicious with a Cabernet Sauvignon from Napa while listening to New Orleans own Troy "Trombone Shorty" Andrews release *Orleans & Claiborne*.

Season pork with salt and pepper. Rub each pork chop on both sides with a generous amount of ancho-caraway rub. Shake excess off. Grill pork chop over medium heat for 6 to 8 minutes per side for medium well.

To plate, spoon generous amount of molasses sauce on plate. Center pork chop on plate. Pour generous amount of molasses sauce atop pork chop. Garnish chop with parsley.

BEEF BRANDON

Beef Brandon is named for Chef and Mrs. Preuss' grandson, Brandon. In contrast to the very young man for whom this dish is named, the beef industry has a very old history in Louisiana. By 1730 there was cattle ranching in St. Martin Parish. When the Acadian leader Beausoleil came to Louisiana, he and 8 other leaders entered into an agreement on behalf of themselves and 200 others to raise cattle on the lands of Antoine Bernard Dauterive. Ten generations later, some descendants continue to raise cattle!

Sip a Cabernet Sauvignon while listening to Marlon Jordon's exquisitely beautiful *Arad's Dream*. Mr. Jordan mentors the next generation of musicians by serving as a faculty member of the Louis Satchmo Armstrong Jazz Camp.

Season beef with salt and pepper on both sides. Grill on medium-high 4 to 5 minutes for medium rare.

Using 1/2 cup of peppercorn sauce, plate by placing small amount of sauce in center of warm dish. Center filet on sauce. Pour rest of half-cup of peppercorn sauce over filet. Top with 1/2 cup of onion straws.

SERVES 6

6   8-ounce filets of beef

3   cups Brandy Peppercorn
    Sauce *[recipe p.195]*

3   cups Onion Straws
    [recipe p.202]

Salt

Black Pepper, freshly ground

79

RACK OF LAMB WITH BASIL MINT PESTO

SERVES 4

1   Rack of lamb of 8 chops, French trimmed
3   cups Marinade
2   cups Basil Pesto Rub
3/4 cup Rosemary-Mint Reduction
1   cup Red Onion Confit
Mint Jelly for garnish

MARINADE

1   cup of Olive Oil
2   cups Red Wine
2   cloves of Garlic
1   Tablespoon thyme, dried
1   Tablespoon Basil, dried
1/2 cup chopped Shallots
1   Bay leaf

This extraordinary dish should be enjoyed with an extraordinary Cabernet Sauvignon from Napa while listening to the song *After* from *Music Redeems: The Marsalis Family* recorded at the Kennedy Center, honoring Mr. Ellis Marsalis with the Duke Ellington Jazz Festival's Lifetime Achievement Award. Proceeds from this album support the Ellis Marsalis Center for Music in the New Orleans Musicians Village. We in New Orleans have always know that Mr. Marsalis is an extraordinary musician, father, educator and human being.

In a non-reactive dish combine all ingredients. Place lamb in marinade and refrigerate for 24 hours. When ready to cook, discard all marinade.

To prepare lamb, season with salt and pepper. Preheat oven to 450 degrees F. In a large sauté pan on medium high heat, sear on all sides, approximately 2 minutes per side. Remove from pan and allow to rest. While resting, rub basil pesto on all sides. Place lamb in oven to heat and brown, about 8 minutes for medium rare.

To plate place a ladle of Rosemary-Mint Reduction in center of warm plate. Place rack atop reduction. Surround with onions from red onion confit. Garnish with mint jelly.

Note: Have your butcher French-trim the ends of the rack.

DUCKLING ANDREAS PREUSS

New Orleans is the hometown of many who ultimately walk on the national media stage. Attaining such prominence is Broussard's own Andreas Preuss. Andreas is the Supervising Producer of CNN Newsroom for CNN, USA.

Savor with a Cabernet Sauvignon while listening to New Orleans' "Bon Operatit's," magical version of *Nessum Dorma* from Puccini's *Turandot.*

Preheat ovens 350 degrees F.

Season ducklings inside and outside with salt, pepper and rosemary. Place in a 17 1/4 x 11 1/2 x 2 1/4-inch roasting pan and roast until juices run clear, about 2 1/2 hours.

Deglaze pan with reserved cherry juice.
Split ducks in half and debone, removing backbone and ribcage.
In a medium skillet or sauté pan, add clarified butter and sauté cherries.

To plate, place a half duck on a warm plate. Spoon deglazed pan juices over pears. Spoon Port Sauce over duck. Garnish with cabbage, onion and pepper.

SERVES 6

3   3-1/2 pound ducks

2   Tablespoons Rosemary

1   14-ounce jar Bing cherries, drained and juice reserved

2   Tablespoons clarified butter

2   cups Cognac and Port Sauce [recipe p.198]

Red cabbage

Green onion spears

Red bell pepper spears

Salt

Freshly ground black pepper

VEAL BROUSSARD

SERVES 6

EGG WASH:

4   whole eggs

1/2 cup water

12 2-ounce veal round slices

Salt

Freshly ground white pepper

1   cup all-purpose flour

1   stick butter

1   pound crawfish tails

4   Tablespoons dry white wine

1/2 cup Mustard Dill Béchamel
    Sauce [recipe p.202]

3/4 cup Port Wine Sauce [recipe
    p.198]

Before air conditioning was prevalent in New Orleans, locals believed that one should eat "lighter" foods in the summer to stay cool. Local "beat the heat" tactics included homemade root beer as a "blood thinner," ice water before every meal and veal as a "light" substitute for beef which was considered "heavier" on the stomach.

Enjoy with a delightful white while listening to Loyola Music School graduate and New Orleans' native Bryan Hymel as Don José in the London Royal Opera House production of Bizet's *Carmen*.

In a medium mixing bowl, make egg wash by combining eggs and water. Pound veal to half thickness. Sprinkle veal with salt and pepper and dust with flour. In a medium skillet or sauté pan over high heat, melt 6 Tablespoons of butter. Dip floured veal in egg wash and sauté. Reserve warm.

In a second medium skillet or sauté pan over medium heat, melt remaining 2 Tablespoons of butter. Add crawfish and sauté. Deglaze the pan with white wine by scraping and loosening stuck bits and adding Mustard Dill Béchamel sauce while scraping. Simmer until thick.

To plate, place one slice of veal centered on warmed plate and top with crawfish. Place second veal slice atop crawfish and cover with 4 Tablespoons of Port Wine Sauce. Serve immediately.

FRENCH MARKET CREOLE SUMMER SOUP

MAKES 1 3/4 QUARTS

3　Cucumbers, medium

1　rib Celery, diced

1　small Green bell pepper, diced

2　Green onions, chopped

1　small clove garlic, pressed

1/2 cup Water

2　Tablespoons White vinegar

3　inch piece of French bread,
　　shredded

1　quart Plain yogurt

1/2 Red bell pepper, finely diced

1/2 Green bell pepper, finely diced

1　small Cucumber, finely diced

Dash Cayenne pepper

Salt

White pepper

New Orleans' rich soil yields an abundance of this soup's ingredients, whether grown in the creole home's courtyard or purchased during the daily visit to the French Market. The French Market, dating to 1791, is the nation's oldest city market. No wonder this soup has graced the summer evening table at many a creole gathering.

Enjoy with a Riesling on the patio while listening to the Jimmie F. Rodgers version of the *The Long Hot Summer* by Oscar winning composer Lionel Newman, uncle of Randy Newman, for the 1958 movie "The Long Hot Summer" filmed in Louisiana and Mississippi and written by William Faulkner, who also often dined at Broussard's.

In a blender or food processor combine cucumber, celery, bell pepper, onion, garlic, water, vinegar and bread and *purée* until smooth. If making extra, may be frozen at this point.

Add yogurt, cayenne and season to taste with salt and pepper. Press through a *chinois* or *tamis*. Fold red and green pepper and cucumber into soup and serve.

CREOLE TOMATO FESTIVAL SOUP

Celebrate the Creole Tomato!

For three days in June, the French Quarter goes wild over this heirloom local fruit of the New World, as split-top ugly as it is delicious.

While you're slingin' a good time with your guests, grab a glass of a Cabernet Blend and bounce to the beat of Yiddish, Irish, Celtic, Cajun punk-klezmer-folk-funk in six languages—that's right, it's the Zydepunks playing *Boudreaux Crosses the Danube!*

In a large mixing bowl, combine all ingredients, seasoning to taste with salt and pepper. Cover and refrigerate 8 to 12 hours. Serve ice cold on a hot day or even hotter night.

MAKES 2 QUARTS
- ENOUGH FOR YOUR PARTY!

- 2 Cucumbers, skinned, seeded and finely diced
- 1 small Green bell pepper, seeded and finely diced
- 1 small Red bell pepper, seeded and finely diced
- 1/2 small Creole yellow onion, finely chopped
- 1 small rib Celery, finely
- 1 teaspoon Minced garlic
- 1 Creole tomato, finely chopped
- 4 1/4 cups Tomato juice
- 1 1/4 cups Boeuf stock *[recipe p.194]*
- 2 Tablespoons Worcestershire sauce
- 1/2 teaspoon Louisiana-style Hot Sauce
- 1 teaspoon Ground cumin
- Salt
- Freshly ground black pepper

POULET LEEK BISQUE WITH HEAVY BAY CREAM

SERVES 6

4 Tablespoons Butter, unsalted

3-4 Leeks, mediums sized, white only, cut crosswise into fine slices

1 Tablespoon Minced garlic

5 Tablespoons All-purpose flour

5 cups Poulet Leek stock [recipe p.202]

2 Bay leaves

1/2 cup Heavy cream

Salt

White pepper

1 cup Freshly whipped heavy cream

When the damp bone-chilling winter descends on the Crescent City, freezing winds blowing off the River and rampaging down the narrow corridors of the Vieux Carré, rich hot soup, savory on the palate, eases the Creole soul.

Sip Broussard's custom wine "Delicato" while listening to the Louisiana Philharmonic Orchestra's version of Mahler's *Symphony #9* with the Symphony Chorus of New Orleans.

In a medium stockpot over medium heat, melt butter and add leeks and garlic.

Sauté until transparent but not brown. Sprinkle flour while stirring constantly. Cook, stirring continuously, for 10 minutes to make a blonde roux. Do not brown the flour. Add one-third of the stock and stir. Repeat twice. Add bay leaves and simmer for 30 minutes. Add cream, salt and pepper to taste and simmer 10 minutes. Serve hot garnished with a dollop of whipped heavy cream.

Note: Broussard's custom wines may be ordered for shipment by contacting the restaurant.

SHRIMP BISQUE

In classical French cooking, the "mirepoix" is a cooked vegetable seasoning base used as a foundation for the dish. Creole cooking constantly uses the mirepoix technique, but never uses the word! Many New Orleanians start Christmas celebrations with this bisque.

Enjoy with a Pinot Blanc while listening to Pete Fountain's version of *Shrimp Boat* written by Paul Mason and Paul Weston.

SERVES 12

4 Tablespoons Butter, unsalted

1/2 Carrot, finely chopped

1/2 Yellow creole onion, finely
    chopped

2 sprigs Parsley

1/2 Bay leaf

1 cup White wine

24 Whole raw medium shrimp,
    40 count, washed

3/4 cup Flour

2 quarts Poulet stock *[recipe
    p.202]*

3 Tablespoons Heavy cream

2 Tablespoons Brandy, sherry or
    Madeira

Pinch thyme

In a large saucepan over medium heat, melt 2 Tablespoons of butter. Add carrots, onion, parsley, bay leaf and thyme. Cover and cook until tender, about 5 to 6 minutes. Add wine and shrimp. Poach for 8 minutes. Remove and reserve shrimp. Cool, peel and devein 12 shrimp, reserving shells. Dice peeled shrimp meat and reserve for garnish. Put reserved shells and remaining whole shrimp in shells into a food processor or blender and purée. Return shrimp purée to

vegetables and poaching wine in saucepan. Sprinkle flour and stir. Add stock, bring to a boil and simmer covered for 20 minutes. Remove from heat and strain through fine chinois or tapis. Adjust thickness with milk, if necessary. Strain a second time through a thickness of cheesecloth. May be reserved refrigerated until ready to serve.

To serve, bring liquid to a boil. Add cream, brandy, sherry or Madeira and remaining 2 Tablespoons of butter. Garnish with reserved diced shrimp.

ARTICHOKE SOUP

SERVES 6

1 small Creole yellow onion

1 Tablespoon Olive oil

1 clove Garlic, minced

1 3/4 cups Artichoke hearts, about
   14 ounces, reserving liquid

1 quart plus 1 cup Poulet stock
   without leeks *[recipe p.202]*

1 Tablespoon Vinegar

Salt

White Pepper

Pinch cayenne

Influenced by the tastes of French royalty, who had enjoyed the delicacy ever since Catherine de Medici married Henry II, Creoles embraced the artichoke with enthusiasm. Long a local Creole favorite, artichokes were a luxury item. Today few realize the first commercially grown American artichokes were grown in Louisiana in the 1800s.

Best served with a Chardonnay while listening to a baroque trumpet performance by New Orleans own personification of excellence, Wynton Marsalis, all of your senses luxuriating in refined elegance and accomplishment.

To a medium stockpot over medium heat, add olive oil and heat until shimmers but does not smoke. Add creole onions and sauté until transparent. Do not brown. Add garlic and artichoke hearts, stirring until heated. Add stock, reserved liquids, vinegar, salt to taste, white pepper and cayenne and bring to boil. Remove from heat and serve immediately.

CRAWFISH BISQUE

While restaurants have access to a variety of fresh seafood suppliers year round, for the home kitchen the best choice is frozen Louisiana farm-raised crawfish tails which are always available. If you made crawfish stock and froze it last season, you are ahead, but if not, do not despair – use bottled clam juice. Purchase a few additional whole crawfish and purée the shells, adding them with the wine to the stock for a true bisque experience.

Experience this classic Louisiana dish with a Sauvignon Blanc while listening to the Good Girl sound of Amanda Shaw, already a New Orleans' classic.

In a large saucepan over medium heat, melt butter. Add carrot, onion, parsley, bay leaf, and thyme. Cover and cook until vegetables are tender, about 6 minutes.

Place frozen crawfish atop vegetables, cover and cook 5 minutes. Remove crawfish, chop roughly and reserve refrigerated unless serving immediately. Add wine and stock. Add salt and pepper to taste. If puréed shells are available, add at this point. Sprinkle in flour and stir. Add poulet stock and bring to boil for 2 minutes, slightly thickening. Strain through a fine tamis. If too thick, thin with milk. Strain through a double thickness of cheesecloth. If making ahead, bisque may be reserved chilled at this point.

To serve, bring reserved crawfish to room temperature and warm bisque. Add cream, butter and brandy. Add reserved crawfish and warm, simmering about 3 minute. Serve immediately.

SERVES 12

4 Tablespoons Butter, unsalted

1/2 Carrot, finely chopped

1/2 Yellow creole onion

1 Tablespoon Finely chopped parsley

1 Small bay leaf

30 Crawfish tails, about 1/2 pound frozen

2 Tablespoons Brandy, warmed

1 cup White wine

1/2 cup Fish stock *[recipe p.206]*

1/2 teaspoon Salt

3/4 cup All-purpose flour

2 quarts Poulet stock

3 Tablespoons Heavy cream

Freshly ground black pepper

Pinch dried thyme

SERVES 8-12

1 1/2 Tablespoons Butter

1/2 medium Creole yellow onion, diced

1 1/2 teaspoons dried Thyme

1 1/2 teaspoons Paprika

2 quarts Shrimp stock [recipe p.206]

1 cup Corn niblets

1 cup Heavy cream

1/2 pound Pumpkin

1 cups Mashed potatoes

1 pound 36 to 45 count Shrimp

1/2 cup Whipping cream

1/4 teaspoon Bourbon

1/2 cup Sweet potato, julienne

1/4 cup fresh Parsley, chopped

Peanut oil

Broussard's served this extraordinary soup as part of its Celebration of Thanksgiving. Chef graciously agreed to provide this recipe to the public. Now adapted to the home kitchen, start a new tradition with this soup on your holiday menu. Make more than you need because this dish goes fast. Make it more than once a year and your family will be thankful all year long!

Delicious with Pinot Grigio while listening to the Cornerstone Harmonizer's perfect four- part harmony rendition of For Your Faithfulness, It's Your Time.

To make the soup, in a large Dutch oven or stockpot over medium high heat, melt butter. Add onion and sauté until transparent, but not browned. Add thyme, paprika, stock, corn, and heavy cream, bringing to just below a boil. Reduce heat and simmer 15 minutes. Add pumpkin, potatoes and shrimp, and simmer for 5 minutes. Purée in batches and reserve warm.

To make the crinkle garnish, to a small saucepan, add a high heat oil such as peanut oil to cover bottom to a depth of 1 inch. Heat oil to shimmering but not smoking. Pan fry sweet potato until crispy, about 5 seconds per batch and drain.

To make the bourbon cream, whisk cream until forms soft peaks. Fold in bourbon.

To plate, ladle soup into bowls or coffee cups for a buffet. Top with bourbon cream. Sprinkle sweet potato crinkle atop bourbon cream and serve.

TURTLE SOUP

Terrapin soup was much beloved by the Creoles. Indeed, Lafcadio Hearn's La Cuisine Creole published in 1885 contains no less than 6 recipes for turtle soup! Today turtle meat may be purchased from specialty provisioners.

Enjoy with a dry sherry while listening to the "New Orleans Dynamo" Frankie Ford's 1959 Top 20 hit Sea Cruise.

In a medium stockpot, warm butter and oil, but do not brown. Add flour and brown flour to a medium-brown roux. Add green onions and Creole onions, cooking until transparent. Add tomato sauce and cook for 5 minutes. Add ham, cooked turtle meat, and parsley and cook for 5 minutes. Add bay leaf, thyme, garlic, lemon juice, black pepper, hot sauce, salt and sherry and mix well. Add turtle stock gradually. Simmer for 2 hours. Adjust seasonings. Serve in a large soup plate, floating slice of lemon atop. Top lemon with minced egg. Add additional sherry at table to taste.

SERVES 8

1/2 cup Butter

1/4 cup Cooking oil

1/2 cup All-purpose flour

1/2 cup Green onions, finely diced

2 medium Yellow Creole onions, finely diced

16 ounces Tomato sauce

1/3 cup lean Ham, ground or finely diced

2 pounds of Turtle meat, cooked [recipe p.209]

1 bunch Flat leaf parsley, finely diced

1 Bay leaf

1/2 teaspoon dried Thyme leaves, hand crushed

2 cloves Garlic, minced

3 Tablespoons Lemon juice

1/2 teaspoon freshly ground Black pepper

1/4 teaspoon Louisiana hot sauce

2 cups Amontillado sherry

3 quarts Turtle stock, warm [recipe p.209]

1 Lemon, seeded and cut into thin slices

4 Hard-cooked eggs, minced

Salt to taste

THE MAGNOLIA ROOM

The Magnolia Room had not been used in many years. In fact, it was originally not a single room, but rather a series of small areas. In the renovation, the small areas were joined and converted to one long room.

Gunite had been sprayed on the ceiling and walls. The team sandblasted the interior and exterior of the building. With the gunite gone, a series of bricked-in arches were traceable in the brick work. "When Sam Wilson saw the arches in the brickwork," said Joe Segreto, "he said 'My Goodness! You've found an old stable!'" Originally there was a cut through from the property to Dauphine Street where the animals left the property and went onto the street. Bricks were removed from the archways. Sam Wilson installed antique wooden barriers in front of the arches. Historically, the wooden barriers were used to keep animals in the stalls. The bricks were reclaimed for the fireplace and walkways. Additional antique brick was purchased to complete the brick walkways.

Glass was added to the arches and a raised floor was added to the first floor of the building which originally had an upstairs residence for house workers. The upstairs wooden balcony was reworked, but the interior second story rooms, although used by the restaurant as storage, remain original, even to today.

Downstairs the sandblasting revealed beautiful "sinker" cypress walls and beams — some of the first cypress brought to the City of New Orleans for building purposes. Sinker cypress is so called because it is fished from underwater. Considered the best wood for construction in New Orleans, sinker cypress is dense, strong and imperviousness to the local indigenous termites. Early "old growth sinker" cypress, can no longer be bought. As a resource it was completely "logged out" and now can only be found reclaimed from another historic site, usually offered as re-milled by a specialty wood firm. Some "sinker

cypress" which is not "old growth" can still be purchased for a premium from specialty mills, but it is far inferior to the original old growth sinker cypress. A beautifully grained wood, the cypress walls and beams of the former stable were just enhanced with a simple sealer. Originally the Magnolia Room was called the Sicilian room. As originally restored, the cypress was sealed and decorative Sicilian stenciling was added to the beams and sealed.

A classic Sicilian hand painted vegetable cart was purchased abroad by Charles Gresham, shipped to America and remade into a piece of fine cabinetry for holding wine and glassware. The cabinet was originally centered on the long cypress wall facing out towards the patio. The antique hand painted side panels of the carts always depicted allegorical stories or historical events such as St. George slaying the dragon or the demise of Pompeii. The fireplace at the end of room was added in the renovation using original old bricks. On the ceiling of the room is a curved wood structure that was used to as a drop chute during its years as a stable.

The flooring in the Magnolia Room is terra cotta tile, often used as flooring in Europe.

In contrast to the Italian Renaissance putti in the Foyer, two bas relief plaques in the Sicilian Room are done in the style of maniera or Italian Mannerism with its elongated forms, intellectual sophistication and artificial qualities.

Two heavy antique black iron sconces purchased in Sicily are ornamented by both iron tulips and an iron pimpernel. The pimpernel, a form of primula that only opens in sunny weather, has always been viewed symbolically. According to Roman historian Pliny the Elder, the pimpernel was originally named Lysimachia in honor of King Lysimachus of

a Wine and Spirits Dinner

Sicily, who discovered the medicinal uses of the Sicilian pimpernel and introduced them to his people. In Sicily, the rare blue and common red pimpernels grow intertwined. During the French Revolution, the Poix family of France, using the alias La Rose, helped people escape and actually left cards with 5 petaled simple crimson flowers looking like a pimpernel. Did the Poix family help nobles like Queen Maria Carolina escape to Sicily? Were these sconces on her carriage?

Some believe the Poix family inspired Baroness d'Orczy to write her successful novel, The Scarlet Pimpernel. The pimpernel on the ancient sconces in the Sicily Room remain a mystery. Because Charles Grisham did an historic renovation on the castle owned by the Knights of Malta, perhaps these sconces are from that castle? Was it from this castle that the Italians, Sicilians and the Knights of Malta launched their joint force that finally defeated the Ottoman Turks, saving Europe? Just to deepen the mystery, the same flower appears on a shield carved into the stone of a 15th century well-head in the courtyard of the Palazzo Centani, in Venice, the 1707 birthplace of the playwright Carlo Goldoni, a *commedia dell'arte* playwright. What mysterious stories would these sconces tell?

AVOCADO, TOMATO & ASPARAGUS SALAD

Serves 6

18 fresh Asparagus spears,
   trimmed

Chicken Broth

1   Tablespoon Salt

1 1/2 cups chopped Iceberg lettuce

1 1/2 cups chopped Bibb lettuce

1 1/2 cups chopped Radicchio

3   small Avocadoes

3   medium Tomatoes, cut into six
   slices each

Salt

White pepper

1/4 cup Buttermilk Blue Cheese
   Dressing [recipe p.197]

The West Bank of Orleans Parish did not begin to reach its zenith until the great Sicilian immigration of the 1880s. Fleeing poor soil, greedy absentee landlords, no access to capital and a post-unification government taxation system which placed the greatest tax burden on the poor of Sicily. The tax structure allowed the Northern rich to live in petty luxury while denying basic necessities of food, clothing and shelter to Southern Italy, especially Sicily. Many Sicilians were forced to flee their native land or starve to death. Because of their extraordinary agricultural skills, the Sicilian farmers were able to coax crops from the poor, depleted, rocky soils of their native land. When finally given access to soil equal to their skill, the rich Mississippi delta, the West Bank Sicilian farms blossomed with an abundance of fresh produce destined for the French Market that enriched Creole cuisine forevermore.

Best served with a Sicilian Chardonnay while listening to the original song *Bada Bing* by Mike Coscino.

To cook the asparagus, put in a large saucepan, cover with chicken broth. Bring to a simmer and cook until soft, about 3-6 minutes. Reserve refrigerated in cooking water, half the depth of the asparagus.

Combine iceberg, bibb and radicchio and toss until completely mixed. Divide lettuces among six chilled plates. Drain asparagus and arrange on lettuce. Halve avocadoes and cut into slices. Arrange avocado slices between the asparagus spears and garnish with tomato slices. Salt and white pepper to taste. Drizzle with dressing and serve.

BLUE CHEESE SALAD

Broussard's makes this salad sing with the contrasting textures of crunch and cream and the contrasting flavors of tart and sweet.

Savor a well balanced Italian white wine while listening to Miles Davis' perfectly balanced performance of *Basin Street Blues*.

Using two leaves of radicchio, make a cup. Into lettuce cup place onion and carrots, reserving some carrots, baby lettuces, remaining carrots, blue cheese and cranberries. Garnish with basil. Serve with Buttermilk Blue Cheese Dressing on the side.

SERVES 6

12 leaves Radicchio

6 Tablespoons Red onion, thinly sliced

3 cups Spring baby lettuces

6 Tablespoon Carrots, thinly sliced

Cranberries

Crumbled Blue Cheese

Basil

1/4 cup Buttermilk Blue Cheese Dressing *[recipe p.197]*

BROUSSARD'S HOUSE SALAD

SERVES 6

3   cups Spinach, washed and dry

3   Strips of bacon, fried and
    crumbled

1/4 cup Mushrooms

2   Slices red onion, 1/8 inch each

1/4 cup Broussard's House
    Dressing [recipe p.211]

1/4 cup Carrot curls

Chopped Parsley

A fall crop in New Orleans, this crisp bite of spinach is sure to bring a smile to your lips on the first Fall day.

Enjoy with a Pinot Noir while listening to Looking for the Blues from New Orleans legend Al Hirt's 1964 LP Sugar Lips.

Toss spinach, bacon, mushrooms and red onion in dressing. Place 1/2 cup of spinach mixture on a chilled salad plate. Top with carrot curls and garnish with parsley.

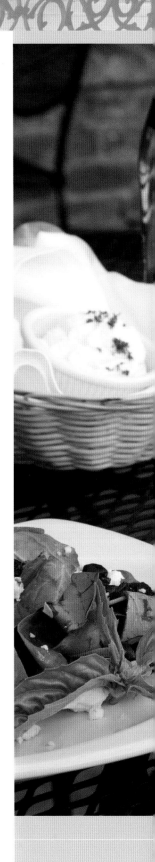

CARAMELIZED CREOLE ONION TART

The "Creole" onion comes in both red and yellow. The most popular Creole yellow onion grown in Louisiana is the Yellow Granex 33 early hybrid, which is also grown in Vidalia Georgia. According to the LSU Cooperative Extension Service, the most popular red onion varieties grown in Louisiana are "Red Creole" and "Creole C5."

Delicious with a Pinot Noir and another New Orleans favorite, *My Town* by Steve Wulff and the De Soto Street Band.

In a medium skillet over high heat, fry bacon until it starts to crisp, about 6 minutes. Add butter and melt. Reduce heat to low and add onions, stirring until all onions are coated with bacon grease and butter. Cover and cook for 45 minutes until the starch in the onions has been converted to sugars and caramelized to a golden brown color. Season with salt and white pepper to taste. Reserve.

Butter an 11-inch spring form pan. Cut puff pastry sheet into a 13-inch diameter circle. Roll the pastry onto a marble rolling pin and unroll atop the spring form pan. Fit pastry snugly into the sides and bottom of pan. Trim excess pastry. Cover with a cloth and place in the freezer for 30 minutes.

Preheat oven to 425 degrees F.

Remove pastry from freezer and fill with onions. Bake until crust is golden, about 30 minutes. Remove and cool slightly. Slice and serve.

Note: Caramelized onions may be prepared a day ahead and refrigerated. Puff pastry is now readily available in grocery freezer cases.

SERVES 6

4 slices Bacon, chopped roughly

3 Tablespoons Butter, unsalted

4 pounds Yellow creole onions, thinly sliced

Salt

White pepper

1/2 pound Frozen puff pastry, thawed

CAESAR SALAD

SERVES 6

3 cups Romaine lettuce

1/4 cup Caesar Salad Dressing
   [recipe p.213]

12 Anchovies, wrapped

6 Tablespoons Shredded Pecorino-
   Romano

90 Croutons, toasted in garlic and
   butter

Parsley

Napoleon often wore a laurel wreath emulating Caesar on state occasions. How he would have loved this salad!

Enjoy with an Italian white while listening to Don Vappie and the Creole Jazz Serenader's version of Skoodle-um-skoo from their award winning release Creole Blues.

Toss romaine in Caesar dressing. Place 1/2 cup of romaine on chilled salad plate. Surround with 1 Tablespoon of Pecorino-Romano and 15 croutons. Top romaine with 3 rolled anchovies. Top anchovies with parsley.

CHÈVRE SALAD

Culinary tourism has always been an essential part of New Orleans, but with the increase of farmer's markets and small dairy farms creating goat cheese and other home grown specialties, agritourism is a growing market.

Chablis and New Orleans own Shades of Praise -- the percect combination!

In a medium mixing bowl, combine lettuce, radishes, olives, beets, tomatoes and salad dressing and toss. Spread goat cheese on croutons. To serve place 1/2 cup of lettuce mixture on chilled salad plate with 2 croutons.

SERVES 6

3 cups Oak leaf lettuce

1/4 cup thinly sliced Radishes

18 whole Kalamata olives

1/4 cup thinly sliced heirloom Beets

1/4 cup oven roasted Tomatoes

Goat cheese

Croutons

1/4 cup Creole Honey Mustard Vinaigrette *[recipe p.199]*

CONCEPTUAL AVOCADO-CRAB ART

SERVES 6

2 1/2 cups Crabmeat

2 Tomatoes, peeled, seeded and chopped

1 Tablespoon Tarragon vinegar

1 teaspoon chopped Chives

1 Tablespoon mixed chopped Parsley, tarragon and chervil

1 1/2 cups Mayonnaise

2 Tablespoons Chili sauce

1 Tablespoon Worcestershire sauce

Salt and white pepper

3 Avocadoes, peeled, halved and pitted

3 ripe Olives, pitted and halved

The avocado was reputedly introduced to New Orleans between 1830 and 1840. Although not native to the area, avocado trees are widely adaptable and soon entered the local landscape. Because avocado trees do not survive hard freezes, avocadoes are not grown commercially in New Orleans, but many home gardeners grow avocadoes with success. Internationally acclaimed artist Robert Tannen and his wife famed journalist Jean Nathan for many years had a 40 foot avocado tree growing in their yard. The tree was originally planted by the prior owner, a cousin of the Duchess of Windsor. With so much history at one address, their home on Esplanade also has another culinary tradition, having been built by baker Joseph Reuther, one of the founders of one of New Orleans' most respected French bread bakeries.

Best served with a Muscadet from the Loire valley while listening to Louis Armstrong's version of Stardust.

In a medium mixing bowl, combine crabmeat and tomatoes. Fold in vinegar, chives, parsley, tarragon, and chervil. Add mayonnaise, chili sauce, and Worcestershire. combine well. Season with salt, if needed, and pepper. Place avocado half on chilled plate. Spoon 1/2 cup of crab into avocado. Top with half an olive.

SCENA POMPIANA

123

CRAWFISH ETOUFFE

SERVES 6-8

1   stick Butter

1/2 cup Green bell pepper

6   yellow Creole onions, chopped

1/2 cup chopped Celery

1/2 teaspoon Tomato paste

1   pound Crawfish tails

1/2 teaspoon cornstarch

1/2 cup chicken, fish or crawfish
    stock

Broussards House Made Creole
    Seasonings [recipe p.197]

2   Tablespoons chopped Green
    onion tops

3   Tablespoons minced Parsley

Etouffe means "to smother" and etouffe recipes are found in the earliest New Orleans cookbooks. As the technique made its way into regionalized Southern cooking, many "smothered" dishes appeared.

Enjoy with a Pinot Noir from Napa while listening to *Muskrat Ramble* by Sidney Bechet, one of the first jazz soloists, born into a notable Creole family of musicians in New Orleans' 7th Ward and eventually influencing an entire generation on the world stage.

In a large saucepan over medium high heat, melt butter but do not brown. Add bell pepper and sauté for 2 minutes. Add onions, celery and tomato paste and sauté until soft. Add crawfish tails. Dissolve cornstarch in stock and add to onion mixture, stirring constantly. Season to taste with Broussard's House Made Creole Seasonings. Bring to a boil over medium heat and cook for 15 minutes. Add onion tops and 2 Tablespoons of parsley and mix well. Garnish with remaining parsley.

GUMBO WITH SHRIMP, OKRA, FILÉ AND ANDOUILLE SAUSAGE

Sassafras variifolium grows wild in Louisiana. Used extensively by the local native Americans, the Creoles adopted the use of ground dried young sassafras leaves as Filé and steeping the bark of the sassafras for a tisane or herb infusion tea. Because gumbo is better if cooked early in the morning and refrigerated for several hours while the cook is busy elsewhere, in private homes it is often used as a Christmas Eve course.

Enjoy with a Sauvignon Blanc from New Zealand while listening to the New Orleans Gay Men's Choir beautiful version of *Silent Night*.

Before cooking shrimp, peel, dehead, and devein, reserving the shells in one bowl and meat in another.

To make the shrimp stock, in a large stockpot over high heat, combine the reserved shrimp shells and 10 cups of water. Boil until liquid is reduced to 6 cups, about 45 minutes. Drain, reserving liquid and discarding shells. Reserve.

To make the roux, in a large Dutch oven, melt butter. Add flour. Cook flour in butter, stirring without stopping until the roux becomes mahogany-brown in color.

To make the gumbo, add creole onions, green onions, celery, and okra to roux. Cook until vegetables brown. Add parsley and sliced sausage and cook for 5 minutes. Add shrimp stock and stir. Bring to a boil and reduce to simmer. Add crabs, black pepper, cayenne filé powder and salt. Cover and simmer for 1 hour. Add shrimp and cook for 2 minutes.

To plate, put 1/2 cup of rice into a ramekin and unmold into the center of a soup plate. Ladle gumbo around rice, placing half a crab in each dish..

SUBSTITUTIONS:

Spicy smoked sausage may be substituted for Andouille, a local sausage made in Louisiana.
One 10 ounce package frozen okra may be substituted for fresh okra.

SERVES 6-8

- 2 pounds whole Shrimp
- 6 cups Shrimp stock
- 2 teaspoons Salt
- 1/2 cup Butter
- 1/2 cup All-purpose flour
- 1 large yellow Creole onion, chopped
- 1 bunch Green onions, chopped
- 1/2 cup chopped Celery
- 1 1/2 cups sliced fresh Okra or ten ounce frozen okra
- 1 Tablespoon minced Parsley
- 1 pound Andouille sausage
- 3 Crabs, top shells and lungs removed
- 1 teaspoon Black pepper
- 1/2 teaspoon Cayenne
- Salt
- 1 rounded teaspoon Filé powder
- 4 cups hot cooked Rice

SERVES 6

18 trimmed fresh Asparagus
    spears

Chicken Stock

1 1/2 cups chopped Iceberg lettuce

1 1/2 cups chopped Bibb lettuce

1 1/2 cups chopped Radiccio

3   small Avocadoes

1/2 Lemon, juiced

3   medium Tomatoes, cut into 6
    slices each

1   jar hearts of Palm, drained and
    halved lengthwise

1/4 cup Basil Pesto Aioli *[recipe
    p.194]*

Mayor Moon Landrieu, father to Senator Mary Landrieu and Mayor Mitch Landrieu, fell in love with the King Palms in Miami and brought them back to New Orleans. He planted them up and down Canal Steet. New Orleanians took to them and soon King Palms were in front and back yards throughout the City. Although occasional victims to a severe freeze, palms are always quickly replaced and like the Landrieus themselves continue as part of the heritage of the City, no matter the weather.

Enjoy with a Sauvignon Blanc while listening to New Orleans Mezzo-Soprano Givonna Joseph, Founder and Director of OperaCreole.

To cook the asparagus, put in a large saucepan, cover with chicken stock. Bring to a simmer and cook until medium, about 3-6 minutes. Reserve refrigerated.

Combine iceberg, bibb and radicchio and toss until completely mixed. Divide lettuces among six chilled plates. Drain asparagus and arrange on lettuce. Halve avocadoes and cut into slices. Drizzle avocado with lemon juice to prevent browning. Arrange avocado slices between the asparagus spears and garnish with tomato slices. Top with hearts of palm. Drizzle with dressing and serve.

JAMBALAYA

This classic is a great "leftovers" dish. Make red beans and rice with pickled pork meat on Monday, poultry on Tuesday, ham on Wednesday, sausage on Thursday, shrimp on Friday and save some each day for Jambalaya Saturday. Red Jambalaya is made with tomatoes, tomato sauce or tomato paste. Brown Jambalaya is tomato free. To convert this recipe to a Red Jambalaya, add 3 tomatoes.

Best enjoyed with a Shiraz from Australia while listening to Tab Benoit's amazing version of *Jambalaya* from his release *Best of the Bayou Blues*.

In a large saucepan or stockpot over high heat, brown pork on both sides. Add enough milk to cover pork and bring to boil. Reduce to simmer and cook until milk is reduced by half. Add more milk and simmer until juices no longer run red when pierced by a fork. Reserve milk and pan juices. Cut pork into 1-2 inch cubes.

Preheat oven to 350 degrees F.

Add chicken fat or bacon grease to saucepan or stockpot. Add all meats and cook to warm about 2-3 minutes. Add onion, green onions, celery, garlic, bell pepper, parsley, and thyme and sauté until onions are translucent. Add beer, beef stock, and reserved milk and pork drippings and bring to a boil. Add rice and stir. Cover and put in oven, baking until all liquids are absorbed, about 18-20 minutes. Serve immediately.

SERVES 6-8

1/2 pound Pork

Milk

3 Tablespoons chicken fat or bacon grease

1/2 pound cooked Turkey or chicken

1/2 pound cooked Ham, dice one inch

1/2 pound pickled Pork meat, dice 1 inch

2 cups cooked Shrimp

2 cups cooked Andouille sausage, cut crosswise into one inch rounds

3 large yellow Creole onions, roughly chopped

1/2 cup Green onions, chopped

5 ribs of Celery, chopped

2 cloves of Garlic, minced

1/4 Bell pepper, diced

1 sprig Parsley

1 sprig Thyme

Bay leaf

1 cup flat Beer

2 cups Beef stock

3 cups Rice

LOUISIANA CRABCAKES WITH CREOLE MUSTARD-CAPER SAUCE

SERVES 6

1 1/2 pound Jumbo lump crabmeat

1/2 cup sliced Green onions

2 Tablespoons finely diced Red bell pepper

2 Tablespoons finely diced Yellow bell pepper

1 1/2 cups Bread crumbs

1/2 teaspoons dry Mustard

1 teaspoon Salt

1/2 teaspoon White pepper

3/4 cup Béchamel sauce *[recipe p.194]*

Bread crumbs to coat crabcakes

1/2 cup oil

Creole Mustard-Caper Sauce *[recipe p.200]*

The eating of crabs dates back to prehistoric man. As for the crabcake, wherever there is crab and crumbs, there is a crabcake. As early as 171 B.C. there were bakers making bread in Rome from flour, water, salt and yeast and the Romans considered oysters a delicacy. The first roman course, the gustatio or appetizer was often shellfish and wealthy Romans were known to enjoy exotic shellfish such as sea urchins. In China, eating crabs dates back to the Western Zhou Dynasty 1046-221 B.C. The main agricultural products of the Western Zhou Dynasty were millet, wheat, rice and fruit. We know that by the Sui and Tang Dynasties [581-907] the Imperial Court served crab rolls.

This dish, highlighted by spicy creole mustard sauce, is delicious with a Reisling while listening to Banu Gibson 's hot and spicy jazz version of *Put The Blame on Mame* from her release *Steppin' Out.*

In a large bowl, toss green onions and bell peppers. Add lump crabmeat and gently combine. Avoid breaking crabmeat lumps.

In a medium bowl combine bread crumbs, dry mustard, salt and pepper. Fold breadcrumbs into crabmeat. Fold Béchamel sauce into crabmeat.

Divide into 12 equal portions. Make each portion into a patty. Dredge the crabcake patty in additional breadcrumbs to coat. Pan fry the crabcakes in oil on both sides until golden on the outside.

To plate, place two crabcakes, one slightly atop the other, dot plate with creole mustard caper sauce and garnish.

RED BEANS AND RICE

Louis Armstrong signed his letters "Red Beans and Ricely Yours" for a reason! This update of a New Orleans classic lends sophistication to every table.

Dig in with a cheerful Gewurztraminer while listening to vintage Dixieland jazz and the banjo virtuosity of New Orleans musician Don Vappie and the Creole Jazz Serenaders. In the mood for a video? Check out American Creole New Orleans Reunion starring Don Vappie and produced and directed by the award-winning husband and wife team of Glen Pitre and Michelle Benoit.

Sort dried beans, removing any debris. Wash beans by immersing in a bowl of water. Bean dust and other impurities will float to the surface. Drain and immerse twice. Put beans in a medium mixing bowl and cover with water to twice its volume. Allow to soak 8-12 hours.

In a medium black covered pot or Dutch oven over high heat, fry bacon. Remove bacon to cool and reserve cold and crumbled. Add sausage and ham to bacon grease in the pan and sauté 1 minute. Add onion, bell pepper, parsley, and garlic and sauté until onions caramelize, about 2-3 minutes. Add bay leaves and lower heat to a simmer until beans are tender about 1 1/2 hours.

To place, place hot rice on bottom of a soup plate. Cover with beans. Serve with a dash of sherry and a dollop of sour cream. Garnish sour cream with pimentos, green onions and a sprinkle of reserved crumbled bacon. A Louisiana-style hot sauce or pickled pepper sauce or jalapeno peppers are optional.

SERVES 6 - 8

- 1 pound dried Red kidney beans
- Water
- 3 slices Bacon
- 1/2 pound Andouille sausage, cut into 1/2 inch rounds
- 1/2 pound Ham, dice 1 inch
- 1 Creole yellow onion
- 1/4 Red bell pepper
- 1/4 Green bell pepper
- 1 Tablespoon Parsley
- 1 Tablespoon minced roasted Garlic
- 1 Bay leaf
- Sherry
- Sour cream
- 3 Tablespoons Pimento, finely chopped
- 3 Tablespoons finely chopped Green onions
- Louisiana style hot sauce or pickled pepper sauce or jalapeno peppers, sliced

SHRIMP CREOLE

SERVES 6-8

4 Tablespoons Butter, unsalted

3 large Onions, roughly chopped

2 large Bell peppers, seeded and rough chopped

1 stalk Celery, minced

4 cloves Garlic, minced

5 large Tomatoes, skinner, seeded, and rough chopped

1 teaspoon Thyme

4 Bay leaves

1 teaspoon Paprika

2 Tablespoon minced Parsley

Salt and white pepper

Cayenne pepper

1 teaspoon Cornstarch

1 Tablespoon Water

3 pounds whole raw Shrimp, headed, peeled and deveined

4 cups hot cooked Rice

2 Tablespoons minced Green onions

One-third of the seafood used in the United States comes from Louisiana. Think about it.

Delicious with a Pinot Grigio from Argentina, accompanied by the music of American composer and pianist, "the Creole Mozart," Louis Moreau Gottschalk who surely walked before the Broussard's building on the way to his home at 518 Conti.

In a large skillet or sauté pan, melt butter and sauté onions, bell pepper, celery, and garlic until limp but not brown, about 3-5 minutes. Add tomatoes, thyme, bay leaves, paprika, parsley, salt, pepper, and cayenne. Simmer for 10 minutes.

In a small bowl, mix cornstarch and water. Add cornstarch to skillet or sauté pan and simmer for 2 minutes. Add shrimp, cooking until shrimp are just pink, about 2-3 minutes. Serve.

To plate, spoon shrimp creole into warmed soup plates and top with a scoop of hot rice. Top rice with 2 cooked shrimp and minced green onion tops.

Creole remoulade is traditionally served with seafood in restaurants, with Shrimp Remoulade being the most famous incarnation. At home, however, New Orleanians, having grown up with remoulade, are known to slather the sauce on anything and everything, including french fries, sandwiches, raw and fried vegetables, hot dogs, potato salad, and hamburgers. For those with less of a creole craving for the condiment, this elegant dish is sure to please the most advanced palate.

Enjoy with a Cabernet Sauvignon from the Napa valley while listening to New Orleans Tenor Cedric Bridges, 1992 District Winner of the Metropolitan Opera Auditions and a performer with the Houston Grand Opera, the Des Moines Metro Opera, the New Orleans Opera and Temple Sinai.

In a large stock pot over medium heat, combine water, liquid crab boil, salt and quartered lemons and bring to simmer for 15 minutes. Add whole shrimp and bring to boil, immediately turning off heat. Stand for 10 to 15 minutes until first completely pink. Strain shrimp and cool to room temperature. Peel and devein shrimp and chill.

In a medium bowl, mix half of shrimp with Remoulade Rouge. In a second medium bowl, mix other half with Remoulade Vert. In a third bowl, combine crabmeat and ravigote sauce. Cover all three bowls and refrigerate 8 to 12 hours to chill.

To serve, chill 6 salad plates. Fashion radicchio into two radicchio cups per plate. Lay Boston lettuce leaves as a flat base next to the cups. Divide shrimp in green remoulade among first radicchio cups and top with three dice of red bell pepper. Divide shrimp in red remoulade among second radicchio cups and top with three dice of red bell pepper. Divide crab among lettuce bases. Garnish crab with 3 capers each. Garnish plates with lemon spirals and a sprig of dill.

SERVES 6

- 1 gallon Water
- 1/4 cup liquid Crab boil
- 3/4 cup Salt
- 3 Lemons, quartered
- 2 pounds whole fresh shrimp
- 1 pound pasteurized jumbo lump crabmeat, picked and free of shells
- 1 1/2 cups Rouge Remoulade Sauce [recipe p.212]
- 1 1/2 cups Vert Remoulade Sauce [recipe p.212]
- 1 cup Ravigote Sauce
- 1 head of Boston lettuce
- 12 inner radicchio leaves as cups
- 1/4 cup diced red bell pepper
- 1/4 cup diced green bell pepper
- 18 Capers
- 3 Lemons, halved and spiral cut

THE DESSERT STATION

Affixed to the front of the Dessert Station is the crest of Broussard's designed by Mr. Joseph Segreto and executed by artists Charles Reinike and Charles Reinike III.

Two chef putti symbolizing the Italian Renaissance hold a laurel wreath, which Napoleon often wore on state occasions to remind the French people that Rome was the First Empire and his was the Second Empire.

Atop the wreath is a crown similar to the replica Charlemagne crown set with Roman cameos with which Napoleon crowned himself at the Cathedral of Notre Dame. The crown is topped with a globe indicating it is an emperor's crown, not a mere king's crown.

Centered is the imperial bee, a symbol of immortality and resurrection which Napoleon chose for himself, having rejected the fleur de lis as it was the symbol of the Bourbon Kings. In 1653 figures of bees made in gold were discovered in Tournai in the tomb of Childeric I, King of the Franks, founder in 457 of the Merovingian dynasty. Childeric I joined with the Romans to defeat the Visigoths at Orléans and joined with Flavius Odoacer, King of Italy and Sicily to prevent the Alamanni from invading. Thus the bee was also of significance to Italy. Napoleon was aware of this history and this is the reason why he chose the bee as his symbol.

The Brigade de cuisine is the classic French structure of a commercial kitchen as created by Georges Auguste Escoffier and published in his landmark work Le Guide Culinaire. One chef in the brigade de cuisine is the pâtissier who prepares pastries and desserts. In Italy, desserts are very important for the Carnival season, with each region having its own special dessert. During Carnival the *commedia dell'Arte* also comes to town. The dessert station at Broussard's combines all three traditions— the classic pâtissier, the individuality of desserts and the drama of presentation. *Bella maniera*— the art of food presentation.

New Year's Eve...

...Cherries and Berries Jubilee

CHERRIES & BERRIES JUBILEE

Here Broussard's adds an upscale twist to a Creole classic. Blackberries grow wild in Louisiana. Early on many a bright morning in the past, New Orleanians from all over the city would head to Chef Menteur Highway. Parking cars on the side of the highway, New Orleanians would pick enough blackberries along the then undeveloped stretch to last the rest of the year. Today New Orleanians pick their blackberries from a Pick Your Own farm or from those blackberry bushes that keep popping up in the azaleas!

Enjoy with a sparking wite while listening to the hauntingly beautiful Samuel Barber's *Agnus Dei* as performed by the Loyola University of New Orleans Student Choir.

To a medium mixing bowl, add cherries, blackberries and kirsch and marinate for 8-12 hours.

In a medium saucepan over high heat, combine cherries, blackberries, kirsch, sugar, and lemon juice. Bring to a boil and continue boiling for 5 minutes. Add brandy and light with a long match. When the flames die, serve over white chocolate mousse or ice cream.

SERVES 6

2   pounds of fresh Cherries,
    pits removed

1/4 cup Blackberries

1/3 cup Kirsch

1/2 cup Sugar

2   Tablespoons Lemon juice

1/2 cup Cherry brandy

BREAD PUDDING WITH TWO SAUCES

SERVES 12

6 Eggs

3 cups Milk

1 cup Dried cranberries

1/4 cup Almonds, toasted

1/2 cup Raisins

3/4 cup Sugar

1/2 cup Dark rum

1/2 Tablespoon Vanilla extract

5 drops Yellow food coloring

6 8-inch loaves stale French bread

1/2 pound Butter, unsalted, melted

Rum Sauce *[recipe p.205]*

Praline Sauce *[recipe p.203]*

Broussard's served this Bread Pudding at the Backstage V.I.P. Dining Tent at VooDoo Experience. Twice nominated for Best Music Festival of the Year, VooDoo Experience, held Halloween weekend, has grown to be one of the biggest festivals in New Orleans.

Best served with a German Eiswein and Paul Weston's hauntingly beautiful *Crescent City Suite.*

Butter a glass 13 x 9 x 2-inch rectangular baking pan.

In a large mixing bowl, beat eggs. Whisk in milk. Add cranberries, almonds, raisins, sugar, rum, vanilla and food coloring. Stir until sugar is dissolved.

Preheat oven to 350 degrees F.

Tear bread into small pieces and add to milk. Stand until milk is entirely absorbed by bread, about 1 hour. Stir to evenly distribute fruit. Add melted butter while stirring continuously. Marinate overnight, 8 to 12 hours.

Spoon bread into 9" pie pan and bake until custard is set and top is golden, about 1 hour. To test doneness, insert knife or skewer and remove. Should be clean and free of crumbs when removed. Cut into twelfths and serve warm.

To plate, pour 2 Tablespoons of praline sauce in center of warm dessert plate, center bread pudding on plate. Drizzle top with rum sauce, placing bananas from rum sauce atop bread pudding. Garnish with dried cranberries, whipped cream, and a sprig of mint. Rose petals optional.

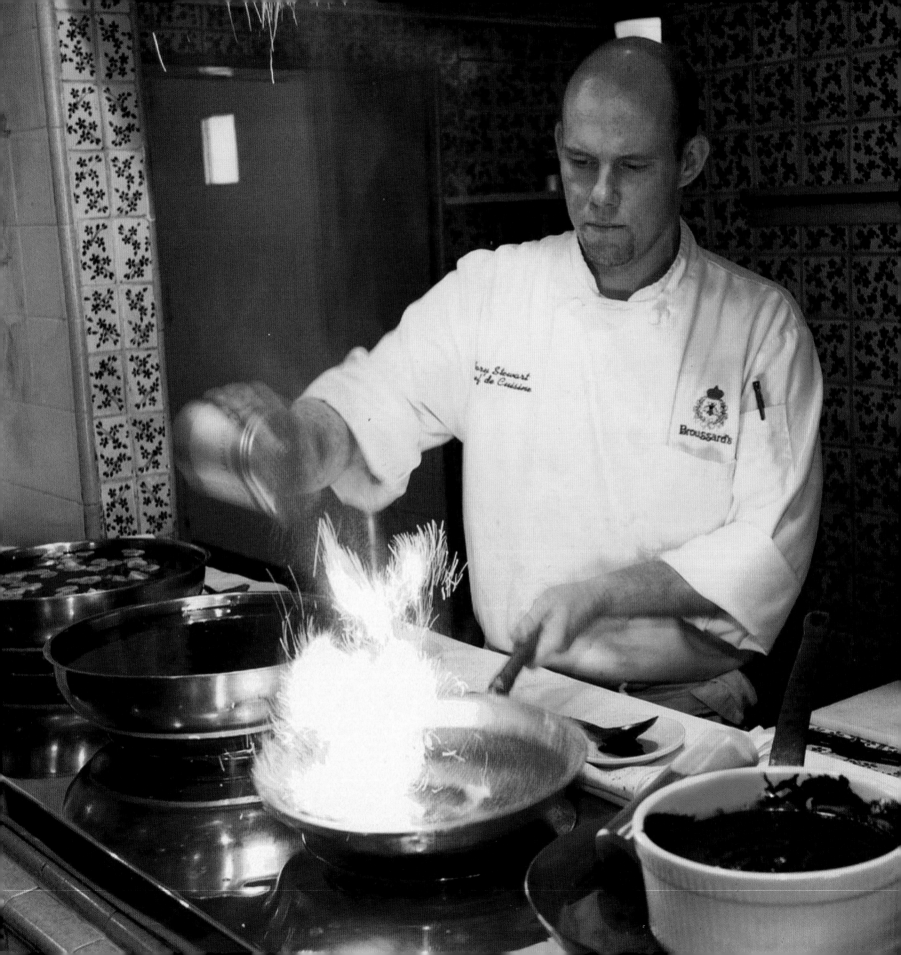

BANANAS FOSTER

French Quarter courtyards are comprised of flagstone or brick flooring and bricked multiple walls. Because brick absorbs and retains heat so well, a tropical micro-clime is created and bananas are grown and harvested in many French Quarter abodes.

Dramatic, delicate, mysterious -- like the French Quarter itself. Savor the ambiance of this dish with a champagne and Rimsky-Korsakov's Scheherazade played by the Louisiana Philharmonic Orchestra.

In a medium skillet or sauté pan over high heat, combine butter, light brown sugar, dark brown sugar. Melt until everything is dissolved. Add banana liqueur to sauté pan. Light rum with a long handled match and pour flaming rum into sauté pan. Add cinnamon and water and cook until slightly thickened. Add bananas and cook until almost soft.

To plate, in a chilled bowl place 1 scoop of vanilla ice cream. Top with 2 pieces of banana. Serve hot.

SERVES 6

4   Tablespoons Butter, unsalted

1/4 cup Light brown sugar

1/4 cup Dark brown sugar

1/4 cup 151 Rum

1/4 cup Banana liqueur

1/2 teaspoon Cinnamon

1/2 cup Water

3   Bananas, quartered

6 1/2 cup scoops Vanilla bean ice cream

CHOCOLATE MOUSSE WITH RASPBERRY SAUCE

SERVES 6

4   ounces unsweetened Chocolate

1/2 cup fresh Butter

6   Tablespoons Sugar

5   Eggs, separated

Raspberry Sauce *[recipe p.167]*

1 1/2 cups freshly Whipped cream

Is there anything better than chocolate?!

Enjoy with Saintsbury "Carneros" Pinot Noir while listening to Groove City by Chocolate Milk, the New Orleans Soul & Funk band.

In a double boiler, melt chocolate, butter and sugar, stirring continuously until completely dissolved. Cool to room temperature.

Beat egg yolks to ribbon stage. Add to chocolate, mix and refrigerate. When completely cool, in a medium mixing bowl beat the egg whites until stiff. Fold egg whites into the chocolate one third at a time and refrigerate until set, about 30 minutes. Serve with Raspberry Sauce and freshly whipped cream.

Evelyn Preuss *(right)* Grand Marshall, New Orleans Easter Parade.

CREOLE CREAM CHEESE TALMOUSE

WITH CARAMEL AND MOCHA SAUCE

In New Orleans creole cooking, " la talmouse" is a cheesecake, but not just any cheesecake, one made with creole cream cheese. Creole cream cheese may be made at home or purchased at the Veteran's Highway location of Dorignac's, another New Orleans tradition.

This extravagant dessert is best enjoyed while sipping a Meursault and listening to New Orleans native and La Scala tenor soloist Fernando del Valle, sing *Romance* from Salvator Rosa.

To make crust, preheat oven to 240 degrees F.

Butter a 10-inch spring form pan. In a medium mixing bowl, combine graham cracker crumbs, butter and sugar and stir. Press evenly on the bottom and sides of the spring form pan to form crust. Reserve chilled.

To make the filling, combine cream cheese and sugar, stirring until smooth. Pour cheese mixture into crust in the spring form pan. Bake in oven until set, about 1 hour and 15 minutes. Remove.

Increase oven temperature to 350 degrees F.

To make topping, mix sour cream and sugar. Spread atop cheesecake. Put cheesecake in oven and bake until topping is tacky, about 5 minutes. Remove from oven and cool for at least 25 minutes. Remove sides from spring form pan. Cool completely and refrigerate until ready to serve.

To serve, using a knife blade, drizzle mocha sauce vertically atop cheesecake. Using a knife blade, drizzle caramel sauce horizontally atop cheesecake. Garnish with white chocolate and dark chocolate shavings. To plate, drizzle mocha and caramel sauce on plate, center cheesecake slice on plate. Garnish with additional white and dark chocolate shavings.

MAKES 1 10-INCH CAKE

CRUST

1   pound graham crackers, crushed

13 Tablespoons butter

1/4 cup sugar

CREOLE CREAM CHEESE FILLING

2 1/2 pounds cream cheese

1   cup sugar

3   eggs

11 ounces Creole Cream cheese

TOPPING

3/4 cup sour cream

2   Tablespoons sugar

Caramel Sauce *[recipe p.211]*

Strawberry Sauce *[recipe p.207]*

153

CRÈME CARAMEL

SERVES 6

7   Tablespoons Sugar

1/4 cup Water

2   cups Milk

4   Eggs

7   Tablespoons Sugar

1   teaspoon Vanilla

This crème caramel is so good, it will have your taste buds dancing!

Enjoy with a Riesling Eiswein while listening to Cindy Scott's original composition The Boy Can Play on her release Let the Devil Take Tomorrow.

Combine 7 tablespoons of sugar and water. Cook until slightly caramelized. Coat the inside of six custard cups with caramel and cool to room temperature.

Preheat oven to 325 degrees F.

Whisk eggs. Add remaining sugar and whisk together. Heat milk until steam but not boiling. While whisking vigorously, gradually add small amounts of milk to avoid cooking the eggs.
When all of the milk is incorporated, add vanilla.

Pour custard into caramel cups. Place a pan of hot water in the oven. Place a rack in the pan and place the custard cups on the rack. Bake for 30 minutes. Remove and refrigerate.

To plate, invert custard cups onto individual dessert plates. Allow caramel to flow down the sides and onto the plate. Serve immediately.

CRÈME BRÛLÉE

Crème Brûlée means "burnt cream" and Cannes brûlée means "burnt sugar"—this recipe has both. The Cannes Brûlée Native American Museum is located in the Rivertown complex in the suburb of Kenner and is often the location of the Annual Louisiana Native American Festival Powwow held usually in November. Members from various indigenous Louisiana tribes perform native language songs and dances in individually created authentic tribal wear. Native American crafts and cooking are also highlighted.

Enjoy this dish while listening to the title cut from *Worth The Wait* released by Gray Hawk Perkins and The Grayhawk Band, combining complex Native American rhythms with New Orleans blues, jazz and funk.

Preheat oven to 300 degrees F.

In a medium mixing bowl, combine yolks, sugar and vanilla.

To a double boiler, add cream. Whisk in yolk mixture. Bring cream to a simmer, whisking continuously. When thickened, pour into ramekins. Place 2-quart baking pan in oven. Place rack in pan. Place ramekins on rack. Fill with water to two-thirds height of ramekins. Bake 1 hour. Remove from oven. Refrigerate until set, 2 to 3 hours. Sprinkle 1 Tablespoon of sugar atop each brûlèe ramekin. Place under broiler or use a brûlèe torch to brown. Serve immediately.

SERVES 6

5 Egg yolks

1 cup plus 6 Tablespoons Sugar

1 Tablespoon Vanilla extract

2 cups Heavy cream

6 Tablespoons Sugar

CRÊPES BROUSSARD

MAKES 16 – 18 CRÊPES

CRÊPES

1 cup sifted all-purpose flour

1 Tablespoon sugar

Pinch salt

3 eggs

2 cups milk

1 teaspoon vanilla extract

6 Tablespoons melted butter

STRAWBERRY SAUCE

1 10-ounce package frozen
strawberries

1/4 cup sugar

1/4 cup water

1/2 cup strawberry liqueur

12 medium fresh strawberries,
hulled and halved

FILLING

3/4 cup cream cheese

1/4 cup whipping cream

2 Tablespoons sugar

1 teaspoon lemon juice

1/2 cup chopped walnuts

Whipped cream

Fresh mint

Louisiana consistently is in the top 10 strawberry producing states in America. Although this high-risk labor-intensive crop is grown throughout the state, most production is centered in Tangipahoa and Washington Parishes among a tightly-knit group of farm families who have been growing for five or more generations. Long practiced in their art, no wonder Louisiana strawberries taste the best!

Enjoy with a French sparkling wine while listening to the best, *Trouble of the World* by four-time Grammy award winner New Orleans own Mahalia Jackson, born on Pitt Street in the Black Pearl section of Carrollton.

To make crêpes, in a medium mixing bowl, combine flour, sugar, and salt. In a second medium mixing bowl, beat eggs and salt together. Add milk and vanilla. Whisk in 4 tablespoons of melted butter. Whisk flour mixture into eggs a little at a time until entirely combined and batter is smooth. Cover bowl and rest for 1 hour.

Heat an 8-inch non-stick skillet or crêpes pan on medium low. Add remaining 2 tablespoons of melted butter to pan and swirl until evenly covers pan surface. Pour 2 tablespoons of crêpe batter into pan and swirl to evenly coat bottom of pan. Cook until edges begin to color and center begins to dry, about 2 minutes. Flip and finish other side for 1 minute. Reserve on plate and covered with cloth.

To make strawberry sauce, in a blender or food processor, purée frozen strawberries. In a medium saucepan, dissolve sugar in water and strawberry purée. Cool for 5 minutes. Add liqueur and cook until thicken Add fresh strawberries and cook until berries are warm.

To make filling, combine all ingredients. Put mixture in a pastry bag.

To serve, pipe filling into the crêpes, roll and heat in the strawberry sauce. Place two crêpes on a warm dessert place. Top with 1 Tablespoon of strawberry sauce. Garnish with whipped cream and fresh mint.

LEMON TEQUILA SORBET

SERVES 6

2/3 cup Sugar

1   cup Water

6   Egg yolks

1/4 cup White wine

5   Tablespoons Lemon juice,
    freshly squeezed

3   Tablespoons Tequila

1 1/2 cup Whipped cream

6   Lemons, hollowed

Shaved ice

Whipped cream

Fresh Mint

Lemon trees grow easily in a pot in French Quarter courtyards. When summer's heat set in, Creole's considered a sorbet more advantageous as it was considered "lighter" for handling the heat than a "heavy" ice cream!

Enjoy with Grappa while listening to the exquisitely beautiful vocal interpretation of *Please Send Me Someone to Love* by 7th generation Louisianian, New Orleanian John Boutté with Conspirare on the *Winter Solstice* release, then listen the triumphant theme to *Treme*.

Make a simple syrup by combining sugar and water in a small saucepan over medium-high heat. Bring to a boil. Continue boiling until thickens. remove from heat and chill until cold. freeze 8 hours.

Combine cold syrup with egg yolks, wine, lemon juice and tequila in a medium saucepan over low heat, whisking constantly until foam disappears. Make sure eggs are entirely cooked. Remove from heat and refrigerate, stirring occasionally while cooling. When cool fold in whipped cream and place in freezer. Freeze for 8 hours.

Place frozen sorbet in a blender or food processor and process briefly to loosen. Spoon sorbet into hollowed lemons. Put lemons on a bed of shaved ice and place in freezer until ready to serve. To serve, garnish with whipped cream and mint.

PLAQUEMINES ORANGE FESTIVAL MOUSSE

The majority of Louisiana's citrus industry is located south of New Orleans in Plaquemines Parish which produces not only satsumas, navel oranges, grapefruits, kumquats, sweet oranges, mandarins and tangerines, but also budded citrus nursery stock. Ground zero for Hurricane Katrina was not in New Orleans, but rather in Plaquemines Parish where over 90% of the housing stock was destroyed, but the incredibly resilient people of Plaquemines, French, African-Americans Spanish, Native Americans, Islenos, Croatians, Italians, Yugoslavians, Vietnamese, and present day Creoles, are all veterans of many disasters and always rebuild.

Enjoy with orange liqueur while listening to Aaron Neville's version of Randy Newman's *Louisiana 1927*.

In a small saucepan, combine yolks, 3 Tablespoons of orange liqueur, orange juice, wine, sugar, and gelatin. Cook over low heat until mixture coats spoon. Refrigerate until cool. When mixture is cold, whip cream until stiff. Fold whipped cream into mixture. Pour into a 9 x 5 x 3-inch loaf pan and chill until set. Fill orange half with mousse and drizzle with orange liqueur

SERVES 6

6   Egg yolks

3   Tablespoons plus extra
     Orange liqueur

6   Tablespoons fresh squeezed
     Orange juice

6   Tablespoon White wine

6   Tablespoons Sugar

2   teaspoons unflavored Gelatin

2   cups Whipped cream, stiff

3   Oranges, hollowed and
     halved, shells reserved

FLOATING ISLAND PRALINE

SERVES 6

CUSTARD

6   Egg yolks, separated and room
    temperature

1/4 cup Sugar

1   teaspoon Vanilla

1   Tablespoon Cornstarch

2   cups scalded Milk

MERINGUE

6   Egg whites, separated room
    temperature and whipped

3/4 cup Sugar

1/8 teaspoon Cream of tartar

Pinch salt

Butter for mold

6   Tablespoons Praline, crushed

Water

Floating island is a classic dessert much beloved by Creoles of the 17th century. As beloved as the works of Edmond Dédé.

When I see you Oh! my Creole love, On your balcony Oh! I think I see a halo, Decorating your brow
— from *Mon Pauvre Coeur*

Enjoy with a Rosé while listening to Reverie Champetre by New Orleans composer and violin prodigy Edmond Dédé on the American Classics release Edmond Dédé: Orchestral Works. One of the "Creole Romantics" his work *Mon Pauvre Coeur* is the oldest surviving piece of sheet music by a New Orleans Creole of color. He studied at the Paris Conservatory of Music and in 1894 he became a full member of the prestigious French Society of Dramatic Authors and Composers.

To make the custard, beat egg yolks with 1/4 cup sugar until sugar is dissolved. Add vanilla and cornstarch. Beat in scaled milk, until completely incorporated. Into an unheated medium saucepan, add custard mixture. Increase heat to low. Stir continuously, until thickened. Do not boil. Remove from heat when thickened. Reserve refrigerated.

To make the meringue, in a medium mixing bowl, whip egg whites with cream of tartar and salt until forms soft peaks. While beating, add sugar slowly, sprinkling one tablespoon at a time, until entirely added. Meringue should stand in peaks when beaters are removed.

Butter a 1 1/2-quart mold and sprinkle with half of the crushed pralines. Place meringue in mold. Cover the mold with foil. In a roasting pan, bring 3 inches of water to boil. Place a shallow rack in the pan and the mold atop the rack. Cover the roasting pan and cook at a low simmer for 7 minutes. Turn off oven heat and completely open oven door to cool quicker. Removed mold from pan and place on oven rack. Remove pan from oven. Loosen top edges of mold from meringue with a knife. Place plate atop mold and rest for a few minutes. Shake mold gently a few times to loosen meringue from mold. Flip mold and plate holding together. Place mold and plate on counter still joined and rest for a few minutes. Meringue should loosen by gravity and fall away from mold. When meringue has fallen away from mold, remove mold.

To plate, place custard centered on dessert plate. Place a slice of meringue atop custard. Garnish with additional pralines.

POACHED PEARS MADAME PREUSS

Chef Preuss named the most elegant and sophisticated of desserts for the love of his life.

Enjoy with the best champagne while listening to Albinas Prizgintas touchingly beautiful version of My Heart Will Go On played on the magnificent Opus 56 organ at Trinity Episcopal Church on St. Charles Avenue.

Preheat oven to 350 degrees F.

In a small mixing bowl combine raisins, sugar, dark rum and marinate.

Cut bottoms off of pears. Leaving the stems intact, peel pears and remove the cores through the bottom. Stuff pears with raisin filling.

In a large saucepan combine wine, sugar, cinnamon, lemon juice, lemon rind, and water. Stand pears upright in saucepan, holding thumb against raisins. Put saucepan in preheated oven and poach until tender, about 10 minutes.

To make raspberry sauce, in a blender or food processor, purée frozen raspberries. In a medium saucepan, dissolve sugar in water and raspberry purée. Cool for 5 minutes. Add liqueur and cook until thicken Add fresh raspberries and cook until berries are warm.

Plate by pouring Raspberry Sauce into the bottom of a chocolate cup. Place a poached pear in each cup, stem up. Spoon more Raspberry Sauce over pears. Decorate with whipped cream and mint.

Note: Chocolate cups may be purchased at specialty food stores. Should you decided to serve without using chocolate cups, you may center the pear in the middle of a dessert plate.

SERVES 6

1/3 cup Raisins

1 1/2 teaspoons Sugar

3 Tablespoons Rum sauce
  [recipe p.205]

6 ripe Pears

1 1/2 cups White wine

2 teaspoons Sugar

1 Cinnamon stick

1 large Lemon, juiced and zested

1/3 cup Water

6 Chocolate cups

1 1/2 cups Whipped cream

6 Cherries

RASPBERRY SAUCE

1 10-ounce package frozen raspberries

1/4 cup sugar

1/4 cup water

1/2 cup raspberry liqueur

12 medium fresh raspberries

SERVES 6

12 Italian cream puffs, split in half

12 scoops Vanilla bean ice cream, frozen

1 cup Chocolate Brandy sauce
[recipe p.198]

1/4 cup Toasted almonds

Mint

A profiterole is a choux pastry ball filled with ice cream or pastry cream. Choux pastry, made from butter, flour, water and eggs uses steam to rise instead of a leavening agent such as yeast. Baked choux pastry can become cream puffs and fried it becomes beignets.

Enjoy with brandy while listening to Beethoven's Third Eroica Symphony originally written to honor Napoleon.

On a cookie sheet in the freezer, place 12 scoops of vanilla ice cream to harden. Freeze for 1 hour. Make chocolate brandy sauce and reserve warm.

Center bottom of 2 cream puffs on dessert plate. Fill with one scoop of vanilla bean ice cream each. Place top half of cream puff on ice cream. Top with chocolate brandy sauce and sprinkle with toasted almonds. Garnish with whipped cream, mint. and an edible flower.

STRAWBERRY SHORTCAKE A LA PONTCHATOULA

Anginetti cookies are Italian drop cookies, flavored with anise, lemon and sometimes an additional citrus. Great when combined with strawberries from Pontchatola, the "Strawberry Capital of Louisiana", home of the Strawberry Festival started in 1971 and the birthplace of Irma Thomas.

Enjoy an Italian sparkling wine while listening to the Soul Queen of New Orleans Irma Thomas' classic *It's Raining* or her new classic *River is Waiting* or maybe *I've Been Loving You Too Long* or *Time is On My Side* or *If You Want It, Come and Get It* or... well after all, it *is* Irma and anything by Irma is "Simply the Best!"

On a cookie sheet in the freezer, place 12 scoops of vanilla ice cream to harden. Freeze for 1 hour. Make strawberry sauce and reserve warm.

Center bottom of 2 anginetti on dessert plate. Fill with one scoop of vanilla bean ice cream each. Place top half of anginetti on ice cream. Top with strawberry sauce and sprinkle with toasted almonds. Garnish with whipped cream, mint. and an edible flower.

Note: Anginetti cookies are available from specialty stores, especially Italian specialty bakeries. If unable to obtain anginetti cookies, unfilled cream puffs ordered from the local bakery may be substituted.

SERVES 6

12 Anginetti, split in half

12 scoops Vanilla bean ice cream, frozen

1 cup Strawberry sauce *[recipe p.207]*

Whipped cream

Fresh strawberries

SABAYON

SERVES 6

3 cups Strawberries, hulled and
   halved

1/4 cup Cherry brandy

2 Tablespoons Granulated sugar

1 teaspoon Lemon juice

8 egg yolks, room temperature

1/2 cup Confectioner's sugar

1/2 cup Strawberry wine

1 cup Heavy cream, whipped

2 Tablespoons Orange liqueur

Whipped Cream

Orange liqueur

Strawberry

This ultralight custard, also called a zabaglione, is refreshing without being heavy in hot summer months.

Enjoy with an espresso while listening to the *Tiger Rag* by Nick LaRocca and the Original Dixieland Jazz Band.

Combine strawberries, brand, sugar and lemon juice. Reserve chilled.

In a double-boiler over a full boil, put confectioner's sugar and egg yolks, whisking constantly until completely incorporated. Continue whisking until foamy. Whisk in wine until volume of sabayon doubles and remove from heat.

Whip heavy cream until forms soft peaks.

Fold whipped cream into sabayon. To fold, combine lightly by placing lighter ingredient on top of heavier ingredient. Using a spatula at the 12 o'clock position of the bowl, slice through center of stacked ingredients, curving spatula around the bottom of the bowl and flipping approximately one-third of bowl contents. Move to 5 o'clock position and repeat. Move to 9 o'clock position and repeat. Do not stir. Add orange liqueur.

Spoon into parfait glasses, alternating with fresh fruits and serve. Garnish with whipped cream drizzled with orange liqueur and a strawberry.

Wines by the Glass

Red Wine

Napa Cellars (Napa) Pinot Noir
Franciscan (Napa) Merlot
Robert Mondavi (California) Cabernet
Broussard's House Reds

White Wine

Hogue (Columbia Valley) Riesling
Robert Mondavi (California) Chardonnay
Kim Crawford (New Zealand) Sauvignon Blanc
Ruffino (Italy) Pinot Grigio
Broussard's House Chardonnay

Champagnes

Mumm (California) Sparkling

THE PREUSS SALON

"I think it's the most beautiful bar in the City," says Mr. Joe Segreto. "The walls were upholstered in a Fortuny black suede so they would disappear. The famous Pennell prints from the 1800s were all over the bar."

Joseph Pennell's sketches of New Orleans were published in George Washington Cable's book The Creole's of Louisiana in 1884. He married noted cookbook writer and biographer Elizabeth Robins and the two moved to London where they befriended James McNeill Whistler. The couple collaborated with Whistler on travel writings. In 1903 Elizabeth Pennell published My Cookery Books, a personal account of her cooking adventures. In 1917 the Pennells returned to the United States and settled in New York where Pennell taught at the Art Students' League in New York City. Their friends and associates included Henry James, John Singer Sargent and Auguste Rodin. All of Pennell's published graphics, approximately 1,885, are in the Library of Congress. The Library of Congress also holds Elizabeth Pennell's 433 European cookbooks. Her cookbook collection emphasized French and Italian cookbooks from the 16th through the 18th century. She also acquired an illustrated edition of Bartolomeo Scappi's *Opera dell'arte del cucinare* published in Venice in 1574 which is now at the Library. Bartolomeo Scappi was the Renaissance chef for Popes Pius IV and V. His cookbook contains 1000 Renaissance recipes and is famous for the first known picture of a fork.

The tabletops in the Preuss Lounge are made of Italian carerra marble with an ogee edge.

Carerra marble from Carerra, Italy has been quarried and valued for statues from Roman times through the present. Michelangelo's David is made from Carerra marble. Mannerist Pietro Tacca is a famous Carraresi sculptor who completed the equestrian statue of Ferdinand I. The statue was cast with bronze from the cannons of captured Ottoman galleys taken by the Holy Military Order of St. Stephen.

The ogee edge is similar to an linear letter "s." The Roman ogee was known as the cyma reversa. The double ogee was introduced from the Arab world in the 14th century and became popular in England as Gothic and Venice as the Venetian arch.

The bar in the Preuss Salon is topped with black and dark green marble and backed by a series of leaded beveled glass panels over mirror. Hanging on one panel is an old and mysterious trumpet. The chairs are replicas of the French iconic Michael Thonet bentwood side chairs first shown at the 1867 World Exposition in Paris. The walls of the bar currently exhibit the extraordinary range of culinary awards won by Gunter Preuss and Broussard's.

With its bank of antique windows overlooking the courtyard, the bar which has internally wired microphone jacks and has often held a grand piano, is a focal point for the many celebrities and musicians who have played or visited including Tony Bennett, Elizabeth Taylor, Englebert Humperdink, Sammy Davis, Jr., Louis Prima, Sam Butera and Sam Adams.

Casual Sundays

Daily Specials

Charcuterie &

The Game

TROUT COURTBOUILLON

SERVES 6

3/4 cup Vegetable oil

3/4 cup All purpose flour

1 cup chopped Onions

1 cup chopped Celery

1 cup chopped Bell pepper

2 8 ounce cans Tomato Sauce

1 1/2 quarts beef stock

1 Tablespoon fresh Thyme leaves

1 Tablespoon chopped fresh Basil

2 Bay leaves

1/2 lemon, cut 1/4 inch slices

1 cup chopped Green onions

1 cup chopped Cilantro

3 pounds trout fillets, deboned

Salt

Pepper

While generally seen with redfish, Broussard's adds a new twist with trout! In classic French cuisine, a "courtbouillon" or "short broth" is a flavored cooking liquid, short of being a stock due to the inclusion of an acid and in time of use and time of creation and complexity. There are many types courtbouillons, for example, the boiling vinegar water used to poach eggs is, in fact, a courtbouillon. Most commonly the French term "courtbouillon" is taken to mean a fish poaching liquid, classically composed of water, white wine, a mirepoix [carrot, onion, celery], a bouquet garni of varying herbs and salt and pepper. The classic "courtbouillon" is not served with the poached item.

The Creoles and the Cajuns could not leave this well enough alone! A Louisiana courtbouillon is still a poaching liquid for fish, but the locally available ingredients known as "holy trinity" [onions, celery, bell pepper] are substituted for the mirapoix. Carrots have never grown well in Louisiana as a commercial crop. In 2002, for example 21 Louisiana growers had 6 acres in the entire State planted in carrots and produced only 375 dozen bunches at a value of $15,000. Compare that to the Louisiana total crop value of 2.3 trillion dollars in the same year! While substituting local ingredients both Creoles and Cajuns added the tomato! Today a Louisiana courtbouillon is a poaching tomato sauce served with the dish. So goes the evolution and adaptation of cuisine!

Enjoy with a full-bodied French red while listening to the title cut to his release *I Am New Orleans* by our own Vince Vance. Check out his great video too!

In a large skillet or sauté pan over medium heat, heat oil. Whisk in flour, moving constantly to make a dark brown roux. Add onion, celery, bell pepper, garlic and sauté until vegetables until wilted, about 3 minutes. Add tomato sauce and mix well. Add stock, stirring constantly. Add thyme, basil, bay leaves and lemon. Add green onions and cilantro. Add fish and cover with sauce. Cook until fish is done, approximately 10 minutes. Salt and pepper as needed.

THREE FINE Cs. Cognac, coffee and cigars in the bar.

THE BROUSSARD'S SMILE

This signature drink was created by Joseph Broussard in 1920 honoring Napoleon.

Best enjoyed in the Preuss Lounge while listening to *When You're Smilin'* as recorded by legendary New Orleans saxophonist Sam Butera who carried on Louis Prima's tradition of opening every show with this song.

1 part Cognac

1 part Mandarin liqueur

1 part Citrus juices

AUTHENTIC CREOLE CAFÉ AU LAIT

MAKES EIGHT 6 OUNCE CUPS

Water

3 1/2 cups water

8 Tablespoons New Orleans style coffee with chicory, coarse grind

Salt

3 cups milk

3 pats butter

8 teaspoons granulated sugar

South Louisiana is world renowned for its coffee, particularly coffee and chicory with warm milk, locally called by its French name, café au lait.

An erroneous culinary myth holds that chicory was an inexpensive additive used to "stretch" the coffee. Until 1897, chicory was imported from Europe to New Orleans, making it as expensive as coffee. Frenchmen began adding chicory to coffee as a result of Napoleon's trade blockade of 1808. Many New Orleanians were sent to the Sorbonne for their education and it is likely that New Orleanians abroad were quick to adopt the fashion of their Parisian cousins.

In Louisiana, unlike colder parts of the country, one never drinks coffee before or while dining, as doing so blunts the taste buds and renders one unable to fully savor subtle, complex flavorings and techniques. Louisianans have highly developed palates, but in order to cultivate such a palate, first one eats the food, then after the meal, one drinks the coffee.

This method of making creole café au lait is from the late Mary Lee Lemann Dalferes of Palo Alto and Souvenir Plantations and J. Lee Dalferes of Donaldsonville and Covington. One could not find a couple more exemplary of Louisiana's traditions —a fine lady, Donaldsonville's Queen of Carnival and President of her Phi Mu Chapter at Newcomb College, Tulane University in 1940 married to J. Lee Dalferes, a Creole descendant of Michel Fortier le Forestierre, the first King's Armor of the City of New Orleans and descendant of Altèa Fortier, related by one degree to legendary New Orleans historian Alcèe Fortier, grandson of Valcour Aimée, owner of Oak Alley, Laura and many other plantations. According to a Tulane Special Collections entry, the Lemann family moved from Newport, R.I. to Donaldsonville in the 1800s and operated seven sugar plantations and numerous other businesses.

Best enjoyed with no alcohol whatsoever (!) while listening to Robert Seago's big band, The Seago Serenaders, playing *I'll Be Seeing You*.

Fill a large saucepan or Dutch oven with 3-4 inches of water and boil. Turn off heat and place an enameled 5 part manual drip coffee pot in warm water to retain heat.

To a small sauce pan, add 4 1/2 cups of water and bring to just below a boil. Continue to

simmer during entire coffee making process.

Place coffee in grounds basket. Sprinkle a pinch of salt atop grains to reduce acid. Pour 3 Tablespoons of simmering water over grounds and wait until it seeps through grains. Repeat until all water is used from the simmering saucepan.

For each cup of coffee, to a medium saucepan over high heat add 3 ounces of milk, 1/2 pat of butter and 1 teaspoon of sugar. Bring to

simmer just below a boil. Combine 3 ounces of warm coffee and 3 ounces of milk per cup. Consume immediately or keep in an insulated carafe. It is preferable to make only small 6 ounce cups so that the coffee will be consumed before it cools. Do not reheat coffee.

Note: The coffee concentrate can be kept refrigerated in a glass jar. Do not reheat the concentrate, which will cause it to become acidic, but combine it in a cup with an equal amount of boiling water and heated milk. Condensed milk may be substituted for milk, butter, and sugar.

189

THE KITCHEN

A Cross Vault ceiling, also known as a groined vault, connecting the Kitchen, Preuss Lounge, Foyer and Napoleon Room allows for full illumination from all sides. Used extensively in Roman architecture, the beautiful and extraordinarily strong intersecting double barrel vaulted ceiling is a test of master craftsmanship. Rabeschi or "running scrolls" of acanthus decorate the ceiling in the classical manner. Derived from Asia Minor, the term *rabeschi* was introduced to the West by Italy in the 16th century. The four walls supporting the vaulted ceiling are each adorned with a flag referencing four countries that are a basis for Creole cuisine: Italy, France, Spain and Germany. Surely no other waiters in the city of New Orleans have so beautiful and meaningful a view exiting the kitchen doorway.

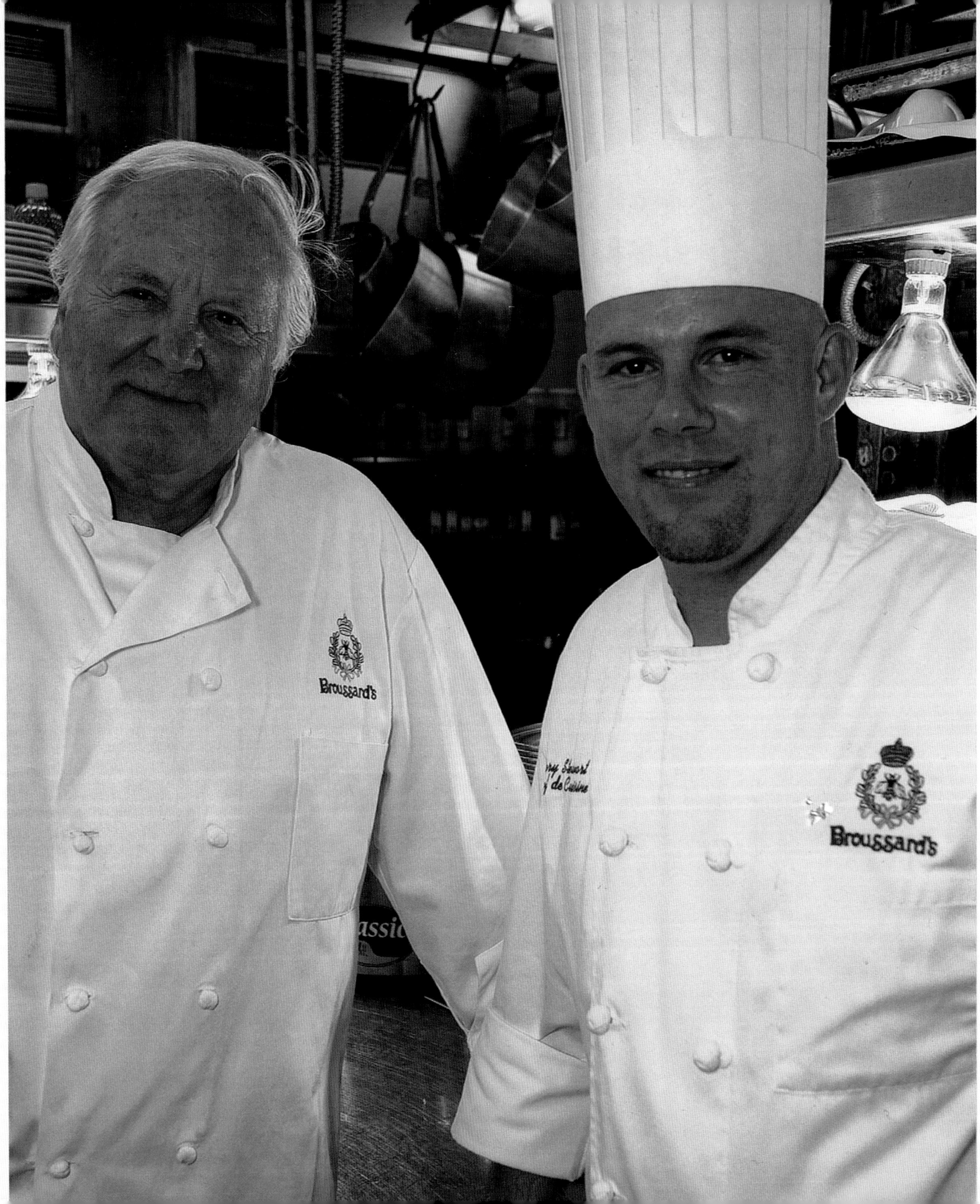

Photo courtesy of the PREUSS FAMILY.

ANCHO-CARAWAY RUB

MAKES 3/4 CUP

1/4 cup Ancho-Chile powder

1/4 cup Smoked Paprika

1/4 cup ground Caraway seeds

Combine all ingredients in small bowl and mix well. Store in dry location.

BASIL PESTO AIOLI

MAKES 3/4 CUP

1/2 cup Mayonnaise

3   Tablespoons fresh Basil leaves

2   teaspoons Pine nuts

1 1/2 teaspoon Parmigiano-Reggiano, freshly grated

Basil will grow like a weed in a New Orleans patio garden! Readily available and luscious on the tongue, basil is now found throughout Creole cooking.

In a blender or food processor combine all ingredients and purée. Reserve refrigerated.

BASIL PESTO RUB

MAKES 1 CUP

3/4 cup fresh Mint leaves, lightly packed

1/2 cup fresh Basil, lightly packed

1/4 cup toasted Pine nuts

1   clove Garlic

1/4 cup Dijon mustard

1   cup Panko breadcrumbs

2   Tablespoons freshly grated Parmigiano-Reggiano

1/4 cup Olive oil

Salt

White Pepper

This is an essential part of Rack of Lamb and delicious with game meats as well.

In a food processor, combine mint, basil, pine nuts, and garlic and process finely. Add mustard, breadcrumbs and cheese and process thoroughly. With the motor running, add olive oil in a thin stream. Reserve at room temperature and use as soon as possible.

BÉCHAMEL SAUCE

MAKES 3/4 CUPS

2   Tablespoons Butter

1   small Creole yellow onion, diced

1   small Bay leaf

2   Tablespoons All-purpose flour

1/2 cup warm Poulet stock *[recipe p.202]*

1   cup Milk, warmed

Pinch ground Nutmeg

Salt

White Pepper

Like its French counterpart, Béchamel Sauce is one of the great basic sauces of Creole cuisine. Easy to make, it may be refrigerated for 3 to 5 days or frozen. Used with vegetables, seafood, poultry, veal and as the base of many other sauces, keep this sauce handy to dress up any meal.

To make Béchamel sauce, in a large skillet or sauté pan over medium heat, melt butter. Add onions and bay leaf and sauté until onions are soft and translucent, but not yet beginning to color, about 3 minutes.

Whisk in flour and cook for 1 minute, making a roux blonde. Do not brown flour.

Add warm stock and warm milk. Bring to a gentle boil while whisking continuously to avoid lumps. Lower heat to simmer and reduce by half. Add nutmeg and salt and white pepper to taste. Strain through a chinoise and reserve chilled until ready to use or freeze.

May be defrosted in a double boiler or bain marie. Whisk after defrosted.

BOEUF STOCK

MAKES 2 QUARTS

1   pound Beef and veal knuckle bones, halved to reveal the marrow

5   pounds assorted Beef short ribs and beef stew meat

2   pounds Veal shoulder

Red wine

1   large Creole yellow onion

1   Tablespoon Butter

2   Carrots, halved

3   Turnips, halved

1   Bay leaf

1   Tablespoon Marjoram

1   Tablespoon Thyme

1   Tablespoon Rosemary

1   Tablespoon Savory

1   Tablespoon Sage

2   teaspoons Oregano

1   Tablespoon Basil

12 cups Water

Homemade stocks are easy and healthier. Commercial stocks are replete with high sodium levels, so put this stock on the burner one cold winter afternoon while the game is on and enjoy for the months to come.

Place beef and veal in a roasting pan under the broiler. Brown meat and roast bones, turning at least once. When browned, place meat and bones in a large stockpot.

Deglaze the roasting pan by scraping stuck particles and pouring enough wine to cover bottom of pan 1/4 inch and scrape again. Pour wine and particles into stockpot. Add rest of ingredients and bring to a boil. When boiling, reduce heat and simmer for 4 hours. Strain reserving liquid. Dispose of bones and reserve meat for other uses.

BRANDY PEPPERCORN SAUCE

1   Tablespoon Butter, unsalted

2   Shallots, chopped

2   cloves Garlic, chopped

4   Tablespoons Green peppercorns

2   Tablespoons Dijon mustard

4   ounces Brandy

2   cups Beef broth

1/2 cup Heavy cream

An essential ingredient to Beef Brandon.

In a medium saucepan over low heat, melt butter. Add shallots, garlic and peppercorns and sauté until caramelized. Add mustard and cook for 2 to 3 minutes more. Deglaze the pan by adding Brandy and scraping stuck particles. Cook for 2 minutes. Add broth and reduce on low heat to one cup, about 20-30 minutes. Add heavy cream and continue to reduce on low until reduced by half. Season with salt and pepper to taste.

BROUSSARD'S HOUSE DRESSING

MAKES 1 1/2 CUP

1   cup Mayonnaise

1/4 cup Creole mustard

1   Tablespoon Minced celery

1   Tablespoon Minced bell pepper

1   Tablespoon Minced white onion

1   Tablespoon Minced green onion

1   teaspoon Worcestershire sauce

1   teaspoon white vinegar

Salt

White Pepper

The Creole mustard and Worcestershire combine for a heavy richness brightened by the vinegar and smoothed by the mayonnaise — a confetti of flavor!

Combine mayonnaise and mustard. Fold in celery, bell pepper, white onion, and green onion. Stir in Worcestershire and vinegar. Add salt and pepper to taste. Reserve refrigerated.

BROUSSARD'S HOUSE MADE CREOLE SEASONINGS

MAKES 3/4 CUP

1/2 cup Paprika

2 Tablespoons Garlic Powder

1/2 teaspoon Cayenne pepper

1/2 teaspoon dried Thyme leaves

1/2 teaspoon dried Tarragon, crumbled

1/2 teaspoon dried Basil, crumbled

1/2 teaspoon Salt

1/2 teaspoon Black pepper

Make your own Creole seasonings mix!

Combine all ingredients and mix well. Store in airtight container.

BROWN SAUCE NUMBER 1

1/4 cup Vegetable Oil

5 pounds Veal or beef bones, chopped into 3 to 4 inch pieces

2 medium Tomatoes, skinned and chopped roughly

2 medium Yellow onions, chopped

3 ribs of Celery

2 cups Red wine

1/2 cup Tomato paste

3 quarts Water

1 large Bay leaf

Salt

Black pepper

In a stock pot over high, heat oil and brown bones on all sides.

Add tomatoes, onions, and celery and brown vegetables. Deglaze the bottom of the stock pot with the red wine. Stir in tomato paste. Add water and bay leaf. Bring to a boil and reduce to simmer. Cover and simmer on low for 6 hours.

In batches, drain, reserving the liquid and discarding the solids. When all solids have been removed, return liquid to stock pot and reduce slightly to 3 quarts. May be frozen in one cup batches.

BROWN SAUCE NUMBER 2

MAKES 3 CUPS

6 Tablespoons Butter

1 cup finely chopped Onions

1 cup finely chopped Carrots

1 cup finely chopped Celery

1/2 cup All-purpose flour

1 cup Red wine

1 teaspoon dried Thyme leaves

1 Bay leaf

2 Tablespoons Tomato paste

5 cups Boeuf or veal stock [recipe p.194]

Salt

Freshly ground Black pepper

The Creoles loved sauce Espangnole which is mentioned in the earliest New Orleans cookbooks. Reminiscent of an Espagnole, this sauce is delicious on its own or as a base for dark sauces. Make it ahead and freeze in one cup portions to dress plain fowl or meats and any meal will become a rich taste celebration.

In a medium saucepan over medium heat, melt butter. Add

onion, carrots and celery and slightly brown. Add tomato paste, sauté for 5 to 10 minutes. Sprinkle in flour and brown, stirring frequently. Whisk in red wine and bring to a boil. Add thyme and bay leaf. Whisk in stock or bouillon one half cup at a time until totally incorporated and smooth. Bring to a boil and lower heat to simmer. Reduce stock by half. Salt and pepper to taste, if necessary.

BUTTERED CAYENNE PECANS CREOLE

2   Tablespoons Butter, unsalted

1   cup Pecan pieces

1/2 teaspoon Salt

1/16 teaspoon Cayenne pepper

teaspoon Worcestershire sauce

Peak harvest season for pecans is October through December, making pecans a special treat at Creole Christmas celebrations.

In a skillet or sauté pan over medium high heat, melt butter. Add pecans, salt, cayenne pepper, and Worcestershire. Sauté for 2 to 3 minutes, until nicely browned. Cool.

If using for Shrimp and Crabmeat Reveillon, do not refrigerate pecans before pressing into the sides of the cake.

BUTTERMILK BLUE CHEESE DRESSING

MAKES 1 1/4 CUPS

1/2 cup Buttermilk

1/4 cup Mayonnaise

1/2 Tablespoon Chopped white onions

1/2 teaspoon Chopped garlic

1/2 teaspoon Green peppercorns, drained

1/8 teaspoon Dried thyme leaves

3   Tablespoons Well crumbled blue cheese

Salt

White pepper

The contrast of buttermilk and peppercorns imparts a syncopated undertone to the palate and the richness rolls across the tongue. Make ahead and use this luscious dressing on salads or as a sauce froid.

In a medium mixing bowl, combine buttermilk and mayonnaise, whisking thoroughly. Reserve.

In a blender or food processor, combine onion, garlic, peppercorns and thyme. Add enough buttermilk to cover and purée. Add purée and blue cheese to mixing bowl and combine lightly. Salt and pepper to taste. Reserve refrigerated.

CAESAR SALAD DRESSING

MAKES 2 CUPS

1/4 cup Lemon juice

1   Tablespoon Dijon mustard

1   teaspoon Worcestershire sauce

1/2 teaspoon Dry mustard

2   Anchovy filets, chopped

1   teaspoon Chopped garlic

2   Whole eggs

1   cup Olive oil

Salt

White pepper

This snappy dressing will get your feet twitching and your toes jumping!

In a blender on high, process lemon juice, Dijon mustard, Worcestershire sauce, dry mustard, anchovy fillets and garlic until smooth. Reduce speed to low and add eggs. Add olive oil in a thin stream until completely incorporated. Season to taste with salt, if needed, and white pepper. Reserve refrigerated.

CARAMEL SAUCE

1   cup sugar

2   Tablespoons light corn syrup

1/2 cup heavy cream

In a medium saucepan over medium heat, add sugar and corn syrup until amber. Do not allow to become red. Remove from heat and add cream, incorporating completely.

CHOCOLATE BRANDY SAUCE

2   cups chopped Semi-sweet chocolate

1   cup Heavy cream

1/2 cup Brandy

Great on profiteroles!

In a double-boiler over medium heat, melt chocolate. Add cream and stir well until smooth. Add brandy and stir. Serve immediately or reserve warm.

COGNAC AND PORT SAUCE

MAKES 2 CUPS

1/4 cup Orange brandy

1/4 cup Port

2   cups Brown Sauce Number 2 [recipe p.196]

Salt

Freshly ground black pepper

Tablespoons unsalted butter, about 2-3 ounces

Created by Chef Preuss as part of a recipe honoring his son Andreas Preuss of CNN, this sauce is delicious on duck, quail, Cornish hens and chicken.

In a medium saucepan over medium heat, combine brandy, port, and brown sauce. Simmer for 15 minutes. Season with salt and pepper to taste. Swirl in butter to finish the sauce.

COOKIES

MAKES 4-5 DOZEN

1   stick Butter, unsalted

1   cup granulated Sugar

1   Tablespoon Honey

1/2 cup Heavy cream

1 1/2 cups chopped Pecans

4   Tablespoons All-purpose flour plus loose flour

4   ounces Semisweet chocolate morsels

2   ounces unsweetened Baking chocolate

Preheat oven to 350 degrees F.

In a small saucepan over medium heat, combine butter, sugar, and heavy cream and bring to a simmer, cooking until golden. Remove from heat and add nuts and flour. Line a baking pan with foil and dust with loose flour. Drop 1/2 teaspoons of dough 3 inches apart onto baking pan. Bake until edges begin to brown, about 8 minutes. Remove from oven, cool slightly, and place baking sheet in freezer. Put baking chocolate and morsels in a medium saucepan over low heat and melt.

Remove cookies from freezer and from baking sheet. Using a pastry brush, coat bottom of each cookie and place in freezer to harden.

CREOLE HONEY MUSTARD VINAIGRETTE

MAKES 1/2 CUP

2   Tablespoons Lemon juice, freshly squeezed

1   Tablespoon Honey

1   Tablespoon Vinegar

1   Tablespoon prepared Creole brown mustard

1/8 teaspoon Broussard's House Made Seasonings [recipe p.197]

1/2 cup Olive oil

Use this dressing with Chèvres salad or as a marinade for poultry.

In a blender or food processor or by whisking, combine lemon, honey, vinegar, mustard and seasonings. While continuing to whisk or process, add oil in a slow stream until fully incorporated. Use immediately or reserve refrigerated.

CREOLE MUSTARD-CAPER SAUCE

MAKES 1 1/4 CUPS

1   Tablespoon Butter

1   Tablespoon minced Shallots

3   ounces Capers, drained

1 1/2 Tablespoon Caper liquid

8   ounces Heavy cream

6   Tablespoons Creole mustard, about 3 ounces

Salt and pepper

Creole mustard, a local product, is more robust that its distant European cousin, french country mustard. Commercially introduced to the city by Emile Zatarain in the late 1800s, Zatarain continues its tradition of fine food products to the present day under the aegis of McCormick & Co., the world's largest spice company. This delicious sauce goes well with veal and poultry.

In a small saucepan over medium heat, melt butter. Add shallots and capers and sauté. Deglaze the pan with caper liquid. Add heavy cream. Bring to a boil, reduce heat and simmer for 5 minutes. Whisk in Creole mustard and simmer 3 to 4 minutes. Adjust salt and pepper and keep warm.

CREOLE MUSTARD-HORSERADISH SAUCE

MAKES 1 1/3 CUPS

3/4 cup Sour cream

1/3 cup prepared Horseradish

2 Tablespoons Creole mustard

2 Tablespoons Heavy cream

Salt

White pepper

Great with Daube Glacèe or any beef dish.

In a small saucepan over medium heat, melt butter. Add shallots and capers and sauté. Deglaze the pan with caper liquid. Add heavy cream. Bring to a boil, reduce heat and simmer for 5 minutes. Whisk in Creole mustard and simmer 3 to 4 minutes. Adjust salt and pepper and keep warm.

DEMI-GLACE

MAKES 3 CUPS

3 cups Brown sauce Number 1 [recipe p.196]

1 Tablespoon arrowroot

1 cup Port

An essential part of Rosemary-Mint Fond, used in the Rack of Lamb recipe, this sauce freezes well.

Heat Brown sauce until just below boiling. Reduce heat to medium. Whisk together arrowroot and port. Whisk port into hot brown sauce . Simmer and reduce by one-third, about 30 minutes.

HERBSAINT SPINACH

SERVES 6 TO 8

2 Tablespoons butter, umsalted

1 small Creole yellow onion, diced

2 pounds fresh chopped spinach, drained

2 Tablespoons Herbsaint

1/4 cup white wine

1/2 cup strong chicken stock

Salt

White pepper

1/2 teaspoon Louisiana-style hot sauce

ROUX

1/4 cup butter

1/4 cup all-purpose flour

Herbsaint is an anise liquor created in New Orleans by J.M. Legendre and Reginald Parker in 1934 and is owned today by New Orleans' own Sazerac Company, established in 1850, the purveyor of over 185 brands in the United States and Canada.

To a medium saucepan over medium heat, add onions and butter. Sauté onions until translucent. Add garlic, spinach, Herbsaint, wine, and chicken stock and stir. Simmer for 30 minutes, stirring occasionally. Season to taste with salt, pepper and hot sauce.

To make the roux, in a second small saucepan, heat butter.

Blend in flour and cook for 5 minutes, stirring constantly.

Add roux to spinach mix thoroughly. Cook 10 minutes. Remove from heat and cool to room temperature. When cool. Using a food processor or blender, purée. Reheat, adjust seasonings and serve.

MOCHA SAUCE

SERVES 6

2   sticks Butter

1/4 cup Sugar

1/4 cup Brandy

2   individual packages instant coffee

1/2 pint Whipping cream

Great any time!

In a medium saucepan over low heat, add butter and sugar, whisking together until sugar is completely dissolved.

In a small mixing bowl, combine instant coffee and brandy. Add brandy and coffee to butter. Remove from heat and cool to room temperature. Once cool, add whipping cream. Reserve room temperature. Do not chill.

MOLASSES-MUSTARD-HORSERADISH SAUCE

1   cup Molasses

1/2 cup prepared Dijon Mustard

3/4 cup prepared Horseradish

Delicious and part of the Ancho-Caraway Rubbed Pork Chop recipe.

Combine all ingredients in a small bowl and mix well. Store refrigerated. Bring to room temperature before serving.

MUSTARD DILL BÉCHAMEL SAUCE

MAKES 3/4 CUPS

2   Tablespoons butter

1   small Creole yellow onion, diced

1   small Bay leaf

2   Tablespoons All-purpose flour

1/2 cup warm Poulet stock [recipe p.202]

1   Tablespoon Creole mustard

1   cup Milk, warmed

1   teaspoon Chopped fresh dill

Salt

White Pepper

Like its French counterpart, Béchamel Sauce is one of the great basic sauces of Creole cuisine. Easy to make, it may be refrigerated for 3 to 5 days. Used with vegetables, seafood, poultry, veal and as the base of many other sauces, keep this sauce handy to dress up any meal.

To make Béchamel sauce, in a large skillet or sauté pan over medium heat, melt butter. Add onions and bay leaf and sauté until onions are soft and translucent, but not yet beginning to color, about 3 minutes. Whisk in flour and cook for 1 minute, making a roux blonde. Do not brown flour.

Add warm stock, creole mustard and warm milk. Bring to a gentle boil while whisking continuously to avoid lumps. Lower heat to simmer and reduce by half. Add dill and salt and white pepper to taste. Reserve chilled until ready to use.

ONION STRAWS

1   small white Onion, thinly sliced

2   Tablespoons Louisiana-style hot sauce

3/4 cup All-purpose flour

1   quart Cooking oil

Salt

White Pepper

Delicious with Beef Brandon or any meat.

Toss onion with hot sauce. Add flour and toss until onions are completely covered. Heat oil to 365 degrees F. Do not splash hot oil. Add onions individually and fry until golden brown, approximately 2 to 3 minutes. Remove and drain on paper towels. Season with salt and pepper.

POULET LEEK STOCK

2   quarts water

4-5 pounds chicken parts

2   cups leek light greens, roughly chopped

1   cup parsley stems

2   medium creole yellow onions

2   bay leaves

2   medium onions, halved

3   carrots

To a large stockpot over medium high heat, add water and chicken. Simmer for 90 minutes, skimming regularly. Add leek, parsley, onions, bay leaves, onions, and carrots and simmer for 3 hours. Drain, reserving liquids, and cool. May be refrigerated or frozen.

Note: To make poulet stock, omit the leeks.

PRALINE SAUCE

SERVES 6

1   cup dark Brown sugar, tightly packed

1/2 cup Water

1/4 cup light Corn syrup

1/8 teaspoon Salt

1/2 cup Pecan pieces

2   Tablespoons Butter, unsalted

1/2 teaspoon Vanilla extract

Pralines made with the Louisiana indigenous pecan adapted a 17th century French sweet originally made with almonds to the available local food. This version is a syrup instead, delicious on any dessert.

In a medium saucepan over medium heat, combine brown sugar, water, corn syrup and salt. Bring to a boil. Boil for 3 minutes to thicken syrup. Add pecans and boil 1-2 minutes. Remove from heat. Add butter and vanilla and stir.

Remove from heat and cool to room temperature. Reserve at room temperature. Do not chill.

RAVIGOTE SAUCE

MAKES 1 1/4 CUPS

1   cup Mayonnaise

3/4 Tablespoon minced Green bell pepper

3/4 Tablespoon minced Green onion

3/4 Tablespoon minced Anchovy fillets

3/4 Tablespoon minced Pimento

1/2 teaspoon minced fresh Tarragon

1/4 teaspoon freshly squeezed Lemon juice

Salt

White pepper

You will be "reinvigorated" by this Creole classic. An essential ingredient in Crabmeat Ravigote, this quick and easy workhorse is great for contemporary life, especially if you use pre-prepared "holy trinity" as a variation. Serve with cold boiled seafood, boiled eggs, or cold vegetables, cooked or raw. A perfect dip for watching the Saints, LSU, or Tulane on TV.

In a small mixing bowl, combine mayonnaise, bell pepper, green onion, anchovies, pimento, tarragon, and lemon juice until well blended. Salt and pepper to taste. Reserve refrigerated until served or make a day ahead to let the flavors mingle.

RED ONION CONFIT

2   Tablespoons Butter, unsalted

3   Red onions, thinly sliced

1   cup Red wine

1/4 cup Red currant jelly

Fabulous in Rack of Lamb with Basil Pesto or any meat.

In a medium skillet or sauté pan over medium heat, melt butter. Add onions and sauté until edges are slightly browned. Add wine and currant jelly. Reduce heat and cook on low for 2 to 3 hours until reduced by half.

REMOULADE ROUGE ET VERT

REMOULADE ROUGE

MAKES 1 CUP

1/2 cup Creole mustard

2 Tablespoons ketchup

2 Tablespoons corn oil

1 Tablespoon minced creole yellow onion

1 Tablespoon minced green onion

1 Tablespoon minced celery

1 teaspoon minced parsley

1 teaspoon prepared horseradish

1 teaspoon paprika

1/2 teaspoon sugar

1/4 teaspoon pressed garlic

1/4 teaspoon Worcestershire sauce

1/4 teaspoon white pepper

REMOULADE VERT

MAKES 1 1/3 CUP

1/2 cup sour cream

1/2 cup heavy cream

1/3 cup prepared horseradish

1 Tablespoon minced parsley

1 1/2 teaspoon minced green onion

1 1/2 teaspoon minced celery

1 1/2 teaspoon minced
green bell pepper

1 teaspoon Dijon mustard

1/2 teaspoon lime juice,
freshly squeezed

Remoulade, the classic French condiment, has a highly specific meaning. Say "remoulade" to a classically trained French chef and he instantly knows mayonnaise, parsley, chives, chervil, tarragon, capers, cornichons, and optional anchovy essence. But Creole cuisine has a language all its own and creole remoulade has many interpretations. Here are our interpretations of Rouge and Vert, Red and Green Remoulade.

REMOULADE ROUGE

In a small mixing bowl, whisk Creole mustard and ketchup. Whisk in oil. Add yellow onion, green onion, celery, parsley, horseradish, paprika, sugar, garlic, Worcestershire sauce, and white pepper. Whisk until well blended. Transfer to a covered container and chill 8 to 12 hours.

REMOULADE VERT

In a small bowl, beat sour cream and heavy cream until well blended. Fold in horseradish, parsley, green onion, celery, bell pepper, Dijon mustard, and lime juice. Transfer to a covered container and refrigerate 8 to 12 hours.

RICE WITH TASSO

1/4 cup Butter

6 Tablespoons finely diced Onions

2 cups Rice

3/4 cup Tasso, 1 inch dice

4 cups hot Chicken stock

Salt

White pepper

Louisiana is the third largest rice producer in the United States. With such abundance, rice often appeared on the Creole table at every meat. This side dish is a delight at the table.

Preheat the oven to 350 degrees F.

In a medium saucepan over medium heat, melt butter. Add onions and sauté until soft. Add rice and tasso, stirring continuously and cooking for 3 minutes. Add stock and bring to a boil. Tightly cover saucepan and put in oven. Bake for 18 - 20 minutes until all liquids are absorbed. Remove from oven, fluff rice with a fork and season to taste with salt and pepper. Serve immediately.

Note: Tasso is smoked highly seasoned pork. Purchase from a Cajun specialty seller or substitute smoked pork.

ROSEMARY-MINT REDUCTION

2   Tablespoons Butter, unsalted

3   Tablespoons chopped fresh Rosemary leaves

3   Tablespoons chopped fresh Mint

2   Tablespoons minced Shallots

1/2 cup Red wine

2 1/4 cups Demi-glace [recipe p.209]

Salt

Black pepper, freshly cracked

Part of the preparation of Rack of Lamb, this reduction sauce can stand on its own with pork as well.

In a medium saucepan over low heat, melt butter. Add rosemary, mint and shallots, stirring constantly for 4 minutes. Deglaze the pan with the red wine and reduce by half. Add demi-glace and bring to a low boil. Reduce heat and simmer until sauce coats the back of a spoon. Add salt and pepper to taste. Reserve warm.

RUM SAUCE

MAKES 2 1/2 CUPS

1   cup Water plus 4 Tablespoons water

1   cup Sugar

1/2 cup dark Rum

1   teaspoon Rum extract

2   drops Yellow food coloring

2   Tablespoons Cornstarch

So fabulous with Bananas Foster, over ice cream or over any dessert!

In a medium saucepan over high heat, combine 1 cup water, sugar, rum, rum extract and food coloring. Bring to a boil. Dissolve cornstarch in remaining water. Whisk cornstarch and water into sauce. Bring to a second boil and reduce heat. Simmer for 10 minutes. Serve hot.

SAUTÉED APPLES

SERVES 6

3   large firm-texture Apples, skinned, cored and cut into 1/2-
    inch wedges

4   Tablespoons Butter

Salt

White pepper

1 1/2 Tablespoon apple cider Vinegar

Especially good in the Fall, serve with Marinated Pork Tenderloin.

In a medium skillet or sauté pan over medium heat, melt butter. Add apples and sauté until just done. Season to taste with salt and pepper. Add vinegar and toss. Reserve warm.

SAUTÉED CELERY

SERVES 6

3   cups julienned Celery

2   Tablespoons Butter

1   teaspoon chopped Shallots

Salt

White pepper

Tablespoon chopped Parsley

This formerly forgotten classic side dish has been making a comeback! Enjoy with Marinated Pork Tenderloin as well as crab dishes.

In a medium skillet or sauté pan over medium heat, melt butter. Add celery and sauté until half soft. Add shallots, salt and pepper to taste and finish cooking. Add parsley, toss, and reserve warm.

SEAFOOD STOCK

MAKES ABOUT 2 1/2 QUARTS

2   pounds Crab, shrimp or crawfish shells, or fish bones

1   gallon Water

1/2 teaspoon Thyme

2   ribs Celery with leaves, coarse dice

3   Creole yellow onions, quartered

2   Carrots, coarse dice

6   sprigs Parsley

6   Cloves

6   whole Allspice

6   Black peppercorns

1   garlic Clove

During the cold winter months, whenever you are home have a large pot of stock bubbling on the stove, keeping the house warm. Anyone passing the stove can have a quick bowl to keep them satisfied and you can make stock ahead for the hot summer months when you don't want to turn on the stove. Because stock does not require much prep or attentive minding, it bubbles merrily while you do other chores, filling your own "little creole cottage" with wonderful aromas and much happiness. Vary the type of stock by varying the seafood: shrimp, fish, crawfish, crab or mixed! These stock recipes by Broussard's are exceptionally fine.

To make shrimp, crawfish or fish stock, into a large stockpot put cold water and crustacean shells or fish bones. Heat slowly for 30 minutes. Skim as necessary. Remove shells or bones and 2 tablespoons of stock water and purée in blender or food processor. Return shell or bone purée and any liquid in processor or blender to stockpot. Add all of the remaining ingredients and cook until tender, about 2 hours. Remove large shells and vegetable matter with a slotted spoon and discard. Strain stock through a chinois or tamis, reserving liquids. May be frozen.

SHRIMP THYME CREAM

SERVES 6-8

1   stick Butter, unsalted

1/2 cup All-purpose flour

1   cup sliced Green onions

2   Shallots, finely diced

2   cloves Garlic, finely diced

2   Bay leaves

1   Tablespoon Thyme leaves

2   Tablespoons Paprika

2   pounds 21-25 count, raw deheaded, peeled and deveined Shrimp

1/2 cup White wine

1 1/2 cups Heavy cream

Salt

White pepper

An essential part of the dish Trout Timbale Herbsaint, this full-mouth, lustrous sauce may be served with any light main ingredient such as poultry, veal, or fish.

In a large sauté pan or skillet, melt butter. Add flour by sprinkling and stirring continuously for 15 minutes. Add green onions, shallots, garlic, bay leaves, thyme, paprika and shrimp, cooking 5-6 minutes. Slowly incorporate wine and cream, simmer for 10 minutes, allowing sauce to thicken. Salt and pepper to taste. Serve as directed.

STRAWBERRY SAUCE

MAKES 2 1/2 CUPS

2   cups whole Strawberries

1   cup Strawberry wine

1   Lemon, juiced

Sugar

1   Tablespoon Cornstarch or arrowroot

1/4 cup Water

Tablespoons Kirsch

Use with Profiteroles Pontchatoula.

In a medium saucepan over medium heat, combine strawberries, wine, lemon juice, and sugar. Simmer for 5 minutes. In a small ramekin, whisk cornstarch and water. Add cornstarch and water to strawberry mixture and simmer for 2 minutes. Add kirsch and simmer for 1 minute.

SWEET POTATO HASH BROWNS

SERVES 6

2 medium Egg yolks

2 large Sweet potatoes, peeled, coarsely grated, about 3
   cups

1 1/2 Tablespoons Flour

3/4 teaspoon ground Nutmeg

1/2 teaspoon Salt

1/4 teaspoon White pepper

3 Tablespoons chopped Parsley

1 Tablespoon Vegetable oil

A great side dish to Marinated Pork Tenderloin, sweet potato hash browns go well with any meat.

In a medium mixing bowl, beat yolks. Add sweet potato, flour, nutmeg, salt, white pepper, and chopped parsley. Blend well.

In a medium skillet or sauté pan, heat oil until shimmering but not smoking. Add sweet potatoes and sauté until browned. Serve hot.

TAMARI-STYLE SOY BEURRE BLANC

2 Tablespoons chopped Shallots

3/4 cup dry Vermouth

1/2 cup tamari-style soy sauce

2 Tablespoons Lemon juice, freshly squeezed

1/2 cup Heavy cream

2 sticks Unsalted Butter, chilled

2 pounds Louisiana Crawfish Tail meat, washed

Tamari-style soy sauce is a generic term for Japanese soy sauce coming from the Japanese word "tamaru" meaning to accumulate, as it was originally the accumulated byproduct of a miso fermentation process.

Delicious on Louisiana Pecan Crusted Drum.

In a small sauce pan over medium heat add shallots, vermouth, soy sauce, and lemon juice. Reduce to low heat and cook for 8 to 10 minutes. Add heavy cream and reduce by half.

Remove from heat and whisk in cold butter. Add crawfish to warm. Do not bring to a boil as sauce will separate.

Note: Do not add salt. The soy sauce contains enough salt for the entire dish.

THREE PEPPER RELISH

MAKES 2 CUPS

1 cup chopped Green onions

1 small Red bell pepper, cut into 1/2-inch by 2 inch strips

1 small Green bell pepper, cut into 1/2-inch by 2 inch strips

1 small Yellow bell pepper, cut into 1/2-inch by 2 inch strips

1 cup cider Vinegar

1/4 cup chopped Garlic

1/2 cup Brown sugar

1/2 teaspoon Allspice

1 teaspoon Mustard seed

1/4 teaspoon freshly ground Black pepper

1/4 teaspoon ground Cinnamon

1 teaspoon minced fresh Ginger

1 Tablespoon dried Currants

An essential part of Grilled Shrimp with Three Pepper Relish, this delightful condiment also works well with eggs and poultry.

In a medium saucepan over medium heat, combine green onions, red, green and yellow peppers, cider, garlic, brown sugar, allspice, mustard seed, black pepper, cinnamon, ginger, and currants. Bring to boil. Lower heat and simmer until liquids are completely reduced, about 45 minutes. Cool and refrigerate in covered container. May be served chilled, warmed or room temperature.

TURTLE MEAT & STOCK

MAKES ABOUT 2 1/2 QUARTS STOCK AND 2 POUNDS MEAT

2   pounds Turtle meat, cleaned of all fat and grisle

1   gallon Water

1/2 teaspoon Thyme

2   ribs Celery with leaves, coarse dice

3   Yellow creole onions, quartered

2   Carrots, coarse dice

6   sprigs Parsley

6   Cloves

6   whole Allspice

6   Black peppercorns

1   garlic Clove

Although sea turtle has been banned by the state of Louisiana and the U.S. as a food source, farming of inland turtles continued for a number of years until a 1975 ban on interstate trading of turtles. Louisiana State University created an anti-salmonella prophylactic treatment and Louisiana's turtle farmers export their crop to foreign markets where the ban does not apply, primarily Hong Kong, Taiwan and Mexico.

To make turtle stock, remove and discard all skin and fat from turtle meat.

Put turtle meat into a large stockpot. Add cold water. Heat slowly, skimming as necessary. When well skimmed, add all of the remaining ingredients and cook until tender, about 2 hours. Remove meat with a slotted spoon and reserve. Drain stock, reserving liquids. Debone turtle meat and grind in a food mill or coarsely chop in a food processor. Store stock and meat separately. Stock may be frozen.

WARM REMOULADE SAUCE

2   teaspoons Butter

3   Tablespoons finely minced Creole yellow onions

1/4 cup White wine

1   cup Sour Cream

4   Tablespoons prepared Horseradish

A component of Stuffed Eggplant Bayou Teche, when served with any seafood dish, this sauce will win the Gold Medal in your home!

In a small saucepan over medium heat, melt butter. Add onions and sauté until lightly colored. Add white wine and reduce until wine is almost completely evaporated. Add sour cream and simmer on low for 5 minutes. Add horseradish and mix well. Reserve warm.

ACKNOWLEDGEMENTS

Thanks to the many wonderful business associates and friends along the way:

The Preuss Family

My great friend, Kit Wohl

My fabulous publisher Dr. Milburn Calhoun

Everyone at Pelican Publishing Company:

Mrs. Nancy Calhoun, Sally Boitnott, James Calhoun, Kathleen Calhoun Nettleton, Nina Kooij, Katy Doll, Lisa Jones, Antoinette de Alteriis, Joseph Billingsley, Adrian Booy, Scott Campbell, John Scheyd, Stacy Schlumbrecht, Terry Callaway, June Chifici, Denise Evans, Richard Frickey

Thank you to everyone who worked with me at Broussard's:

Mr. Russell Civello, Chef Tory Stewart, Chef Chad Haygood, Chef Anthony Rodriguez, Mrs. Van, Mr. Everett, Mr. Mike, Mr. Rene, Mrs. Norita, Mrs. Rita, Mrs. Marion, Ms. Margaret, Mrs. Sheryl, Mrs. Sarah, Mr. Orlando, Mr. "Dark Angel" Gregory.

Thanks to Brad Growden and Shawn Ringen — you guys rock!!

Photo credits:

Thanks to the Preuss family for the family photos.

John Snell. Thank you John for the New Orleans Ring of Lights used as Endpapers and for the Fireworks on page 144.

Fine Art Exposures. Thank you for your wedding shots, Orchid Spray on pages 20 and 21 and Wedding Table Orchid Spray on page 25 and Napoleon Dining Room on page 27.

David Punch. Thank you David for the Napoleonic Chess Set photo at page 183.

Robert Crowe. Thank you Bob for the Broussard's Flaming Dessert photo at page 148.

Ann Benoit - Cover, Opposite Title, Opposite Walk Through, Napoleon figure, Pgs. 1, 5, 9, 11-12, 14A,14B, 15, 17, 22-23, 41, 46, 50-51, 57, 66, 74, 77, 87, 91, 96, 103-107, 109-111, 115-116, 120, 123, 129, 140-141, 148, 151-152, 155-156, 161-162, 165-166, 173-182, 185-187, 189-192.

Janine Joffe - All the rest of the photography. Janine - Thanks for all the hard work!

The Better Book Club: Ann Duke, Ann Hall, Pat Oliphant, Meg Hulley Frazier, Rosie Hines; NPAS, Webb Williams, Elizabeth Schindler, Jamie & Mike Coscino, Sam Adams, Adolphe Ringen, Maurice Le Gardeur "The Bard of Boston Street", Bob and Judy Seago, Mimi Nothacker of the St. Tammany Parish Library, William Chris Smith of the Jefferson Parish Library, Nola Flora, Harold Applewhite of Harold's. My Camera Buff and Art friends Angel, Mel, Bill Schutten, David Punch, The St. Tammany Art Association, Roberta Bruck, Roberta Carrow-Jackson & The Objector Snark, Edd & Lo Frisby, Jodie Flowers, Jackie Warden, John Preble, Yvette Williams and Caveat Eator Dinner Club.

Lexy Frazier.

The Congregation at Northcross which has consistently taught and supported me, especially the members of the 11 Worship Choir, the Praise Band and Rev. Lamar and Mrs. Erin Oliver and Choir Director Dave and Mrs. Melanie Golden.

Winn Dixie Mr. Rodney, Mr. Curley, Mr. Brian Brocato, Joy, Clint, Kevin, Gladys, Jim, Ann Marcia, Evelyn, Amy, Charlotte, Theresa, Janet, Christina, Danny, Craig, Mike, Bridget, Adriana, Ashley, Adrian, Aaron, William, Gregory, Charlie, Gerald, Gerard, Joy, Christina, Jessica, "The Ladies" and the one and only Walter.

When you have your Broussard's Dinner, google and let us know how much you loved it!

Founder Joseph Cesar Broussard.

212